WHAT A YEAR IT WAS!

1959

A walk back in time to revisit
what life was like in the year that
has special meaning for you...

*Congratulations
and
Best Wishes*

To

From

DEDICATION

To Jack Nadel:
My Deep Gratitude For Your
Guidance, Friendship And Support.

Designers • Peter Hess & Marguerite Jones
Research and Special Segments Writer • Laurie Cohn

CONTENTS

CONTENTS

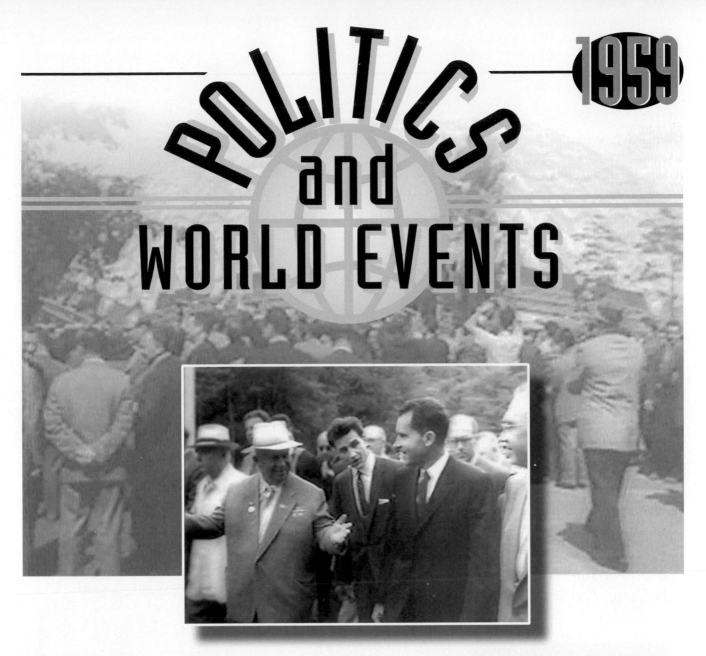

Vice-President Richard Nixon *(right)* is accompanied by Soviet Premier Nikita Khrushchev *(far left)* on his visit to the United States Exhibition in Moscow.

Nixon's free-swinging kitchen debate sets the stage for Mr. K's tour of the United States. Later, Mr. Nixon meets privately for 5 1/2 hours with the Soviet Premier at his country home outside of Moscow.

Khrushchev is greeted in Washington, D.C. by President Eisenhower.

For a whirlwind two weeks, Khrushchev and his moods dominate the news leaving no doubt as to his toughness and his faith in the future of communism.

The Berlin crisis Khrushchev provoked fades when he and President Eisenhower meet for summit talks at Camp David.

CAMP DAVID

Relations with the Soviets and the free world take on a more amiable tone after the talks at Camp David but the underlying realities are unchanged—notably the Soviet drive to match American technology.

AT TALKS BEING HELD IN GENEVA, THE UNITED STATES AND GREAT BRITAIN OFFER THE SOVIETS GUARANTEES FOR IMPARTIAL INTERNATIONAL CONTROL OF TEST BAN.

THE SOVIETS CLAIM GREATER POWER IN VIEW OF THEIR ROCKET SUCCESS.

TWO SOVIET MIG JET FIGHTERS ATTACK NAVY PATROL PLANE OVER SEA OF JAPAN ACCORDING TO U. S. DEFENSE DEPARTMENT.

APPEARING ON RUSSIAN TELEVISION, VICE-PRESIDENT RICHARD NIXON ASSERTS END OF FEAR DEPENDS ON SOVIET POLICIES.

SOVIET PREMIER KHRUSHCHEV RETURNS TO MOSCOW AFTER SUCCESSFUL TALKS WITH PRESIDENT EISENHOWER WHERE THEY REPORTED TO HAVE REACHED UNDERSTANDINGS THAT WOULD RELIEVE WORLD TENSION.

SOVIETS REFUSE NIXON VISIT TO MISSILE PLANT.

WHAT A YEAR IT WAS!

1959

Nikita Khrushchev

Soviets Sign Pact With Peking
To Aid In Chinese Industrial Expansion.

Leningrad

Moscow

Kiev

U.S.S.R.

Khrushchev Presides Over Newly-Formed Hungarian Party Congress.

U.S.S.R. And East Germany Sign 6-Year Trade Treaty
Claiming It To Be The Biggest In History.

Western Plan For Big Four Parley On Germany Rejected By The Soviets.

In His First Post-War Visit, Britain's Prime Minister Anthony Eden Visits The Soviet Union To Discuss Trade And Cultural Exchanges.

Khrushchev Gets Quiet Welcome On State Visit To America.

WHAT A YEAR IT WAS!

*Whatever car you have in mind ...
you're better off with a Buick!*

Almost any new American car you're thinking of buying falls within reach of today's Buick price range.

And when this same money pays for a Buick, today more than ever before it brings you things you just can't buy elsewhere!

It pays for a very special feeling of wisdom and pride. It pays for the magic in the Buick name itself—a sense of quality, tradition, reliability. And it pays—in ways you can touch and feel—for the most exciting beauty, the most advanced and expert performance ever built into Buick cars.

If you're thinking of buying a car, don't fail to see your Quality Buick Dealer. He has some wonderful new surprises for your money.

New Magic-Mirror finishes • New super-quiet Bodies by Fisher • Safety PLATE Glass all around • New Equipoise ride • New fin-cooled brakes, front and rear • Aluminum front brake drums • Thriftier, higher compression, more powerful Wildcat engines • New electric windshield wipers • New Buick Easy Power Steering* • Exclusive Twin-Turbine and Triple-Turbine transmissions* • New Automatic heat and fresh air control*.

(*Optional at extra cost on certain models.)

Le SABRE *The thriftiest Buick*   **INVICTA** *The most spirited Buick*   **ELECTRA** *The most luxurious Buick*

BUICK MOTOR DIVISION, GENERAL MOTORS CORPORATION

THE CAR: BUICK '59

1959

Cuban Rebel Leader FIDEL CASTRO Overthrows The **Fulgencio Batista Government** Replacing Him With **Manuel Urrutia** As Provisional President. **Batista** Flees Cuba.

- Castro Named Head Of Cuban Army.
- Fidel Castro Sworn In As Cuban Premier.

Former Argentine Physician, **ERNESTO "CHE" GUEVARA,** Is Appointed President Of The National Bank Of Cuba.

☆ Havana

Fidel Castro

Castro Eligible For Presidency As Electoral Age Is Reduced To 30.

Over 4,500 People Arrested In Cuba As The Castro Government Launches Counter-Offensive Against Anti-Castro Elements.

Due To "Moral Differences" With Cuba's President Urrutia, Castro Resigns As Premier But Cabinet Refuses To Accept Resignation.

Five Cuban Cabinet Ministers Resign In Protest Over Castro's Agrarian Reform Bill Which Calls For The Confiscation Of Thousands Of Acres Of Cuban And Foreign-Owned Property.

Cuban Government Seizes Control Of U.S.-Owned Cuban Telephone Company.

Cuban Exiles Arrested In U. S. After They're Caught Loading Bombs On A Cuban-Bound Plane.

New Cuban Government Receives U. S. Recognition.

Castro Accuses U. S. Of Bombing Havana.

U.S. Accuses Cuba Of Jeopardizing Relations.

Castro Refuses To Pledge Support To U. S. In Cold War Against Soviets.

U. S. Opposes Sale Of British Jets To Cuba.

During His U. S. Visit, Cuban Premier Fidel Castro Denies Being A Communist In Speech Given To The American Society Of Newspaper Editors.

Cuba Severs Diplomatic Relations With Dominican Republic.

CUBA 1959

Castro and his troops are welcomed by a wildly jubilant crowd following his incredible victory over Batista.

Through the months that follow, the leftist course of his social reforms rouse new opposition. Discontent spreads through the Caribbean and Castro lashes out at his critics with court-martials at home and furious denunciation of U.S. policies. At year's end, Cuba remains a scene of unrest.

Boy denounces Batista supporter.

The tribunal listens to accusations.

Laos, a strategic key to Southeast Asia's richest area, is attacked by guerilla forces from communist Vietnam, a Chinese puppet state.

China's mobilization and aggressiveness cause mounting concern.

Leading Theoretician Liu Shao-chi Is Elected Chairman By China's National People's Congress Succeeding **Mao Tse-tung** Who Remains On As Head Of The Communist Party.

Nikita Khrushchev Arrives In Peking To Observe A Huge Display Of Military Might Commemorating Communist China's Tenth Anniversary.

Mao Tse-tung

Mongolia

☆ Ulaan Baatar

China

Peking ☆

Seoul ☆ Korea

Shanghai ☆

Japan

☆ Tokyo

Tibet

Nepal

India

☆ Calcutta

☆ Bombay

Burma

Laos ☆ Hanoi

Vietnam

Thailand

Rangoon ☆

Bangkok ☆

Cambodia

Phnom Penh ☆ ☆ Saigon

Philippines

Manila ☆

Ceylon

☆ Singapore

Japanese Demonstrators Protest Signing Of Sino-American Defense Treaty.

Communist China Barred Entry To U. N. For 9th Consecutive Year.

Ex-Emperor Of China And Japanese Puppet State Manchukuo, **Henry Pu Yi**, Receives Pardon From Communist China.

Readying Supply Lines On The Ho Chi Minh Trail, Hanoi Takes Control Of The Growing Communist Rebellion In South Vietnam.

In Preparation For Attack, North Vietnam Troops Join Forces With The Pathet Lao In Laos. Ike Steps Up Financial Aid To Laotian Government.

Singapore Gets Self-Rule And Holds First Elections.

King Mahendra Opens Nepal's First Elected Parliament.

PLEASE...<u>PLEASE</u> LET US GET IN A WORD ABOUT THIS

fresh, clean taste!

Copyright 1959 by The Seven-Up Company

Nothing does it like Seven-Up

...we won't take a minute...just have to point out...most popular invention next to the telephone is 7-Up...
sparkles like crazy...tastes too fresh and clean for words...even leaves your mouth feeling fresh and clean when you
finish the bottle! YOU ALREADY KNOW? Pardon us! "FRESH UP" WITH SEVEN-UP

14

Tibet

India

✸ **CELEBRATION OF THE TIBETAN NEW YEAR** Turns Into Bloody Fighting in Lhasa As The Chinese Move To Arrest The Dalai Lama Who Is Rumored To Have Fled To India. Following The Death Of 2,000 Troops, Chinese Reinforcements Stop The Rebellion.

✸ **CHINESE PREMIER CHOU EN-LAI** Claims Dalai Lama Victim Of Indian Kidnapping.

✸ **DALAI LAMA ASKS UNITED NATIONS** For Intervention Against Chinese Occupation Of Tibet.

✸ **PANCHEN LAMA IS APPOINTED NEW RULER OF TIBET** As Communist China Dissolves The Tibetan Local Government Of The Dalai Lama.

✸ **THE DALAI LAMA TO LIVE IN MUSSOORIE,** According To An Announcement Made By The Indian Foreign Ministry.

✸ **INDIAN PRIME MINISTER NEHRU** Accuses Communist China Of Violating Trade And Travel Agreement Between India And Tibet.

✸ **INDIAN PRIME MINISTER NEHRU CRITICIZES INDIAN COMMUNISTS** For Supporting Communist China's Suppression Of Tibetan Revolt.

✸ **INDIA DISPATCHES SOLDIERS To** Tibet Border To Prevent Chinese Advance Into India.

✸ **INDIAN PRIME MINISTER JAWAHARLAL NEHRU'S ONLY DAUGHTER,** Indira Gandhi, Is Elected President Of The Congress Party.

Jawaharlal Nehru

1959

President Eisenhower

returns to Washington after his historic 11-nation tour spanning three continents where he delivered his American message of *"peace and friendship in freedom."*

Ike receives a tumultuous welcome on his arrival in Paris.

Following Alaska, And After Petitioning 17 Times For Statehood, President Eisenhower Proclaims A Jubilant Hawaii The 50th State Of The Union.

WHAT A YEAR IT WAS!

Ike Signs Bill Making Alaska The 49th State. New Flag With Seven Rows Of Seven Stars To Become Official July 4th.

President Eisenhower Submits To Congress Special 7-Point Civil Rights Program Including Support And Encouragement For School Integration.

President Eisenhower Tells Congress He Will Send Nuclear Arms To Greece.

Federal Debt Ceiling Raised To $295 Billion By President Eisenhower.

U. S. Congress Urged By Ike To Approve His Program For Economic, Military And Technical Aid To Foreign Nations Next Year.

Former Atomic Energy Chairman, Lewis L. Strauss, Denied Confirmation As Secretary Of Commerce – The First Cabinet Rejection In 34 Years.

Potter Stewart Confirmed As Associate Justice Of The Supreme Court.

Vice-President Richard Nixon Named Chairman Of Permanent Cabinet Committee On Price Stability For Economic Growth.

At The Urging Of Her Husband, Henry R. Luce, Editor-in-Chief Of Time, Life And Fortune, Newly Appointed Ambassador To Brazil, Clare Boothe Luce, Resigns As A Result Of Attacks On Her By Senator Wayne Morse Who Called Her "Unqualified" And "Emotionally Unstable," Stating That He Had Destroyed The Climate Of Goodwill Necessary For Making Her Work Successful.

For The First Time In 26 Years A Democrat – Gaylord A. Nelson – Takes Office As Governor Of Wisconsin.

Senator Hubert H. Humphrey Throws Hat Into Bid For Democratic Presidential Nomination Along With Senators Stuart Symington Of Missouri, John F. Kennedy Of Massachusetts And Majority Leader Lyndon B. Johnson.

Senator John F. Kennedy Proposes Labor Bill Aimed At Driving Out Racketeers.

Senator From Texas, Lyndon Johnson, Throws All His Support Behind The Passage Of The Civil Rights Bill.

Texas Democrat **Sam Rayburn** Elected Speaker Of The House For 9th Term At Convening Of 86th Congress In Washington. Just Before Opening Session, He Celebrates His 77th Birthday.

Senator J. William Fulbright Succeeds Chairman Of Senate Foreign Relations Committee, Theodore Green, 91, Oldest Person To Serve In U. S. Congress.

Louisiana Governor Earl K. Long Committed To State Mental Institution – Lt. Governor Luther Frazar Takes Over As Acting Governor.

William B. Franke Named Successor To Thomas S. Gates, Jr. As Secretary Of The Navy.

During Investigation Of Damaged Transoceanic Cables, U. S. Navy Boards U.S.S.R. Fishing Trawler Off Coast Of Newfoundland.

Secretary Of State John Foster Dulles Resigns Due To Poor Health – Ike Names Christian Herter To The Post.

PASSINGS

World War II Chief of Staff, Nobel Prize Winning Former Secretary Of State And Secretary Of Defense, General **George C. Marshall**, Who Created The Economic Recovery Strategy Known As The Marshall Plan Which Helped Revitalize Europe After World War II, Dies At Age 78.

Admiral **William Halsey**, Whose Tactics Helped Force The Japanese To Surrender During World War II, Dies At Age 76.

Edmund G. "Pat" Brown Begins Term As Governor Of California.

Edmund Muskie Begins Serving As Senator From Maine.

Democratic National Committee Votes To Hold 1960 Convention In Los Angeles, California.

18

WHAT A YEAR IT WAS!

The Sparkle Corps

You're looking at one of our new Service Station Inspection Teams. These ten women—plus a corps of men—visit Union Oil Stations regularly.

They check the rest rooms to make sure they're as spotless as you expect them to be. They check the entire station to make sure it's clean and safe.

We began this new service to reinforce the Union Oil dealer's day-to-day housekeeping because we know a safe station and a clean rest room are as important to you as the finest gasoline and service.

YOUR COMMENTS INVITED. *Write: Chairman of the Board, Union Oil Company, Union Oil Center, Los Angeles 17, California.*

Union Oil Company OF CALIFORNIA

MANUFACTURERS OF ROYAL TRITON, THE AMAZING PURPLE MOTOR OIL

Nixon in Poland

Despite lack of notice in the press of the Vice-President's schedule, 25,000 Poles line the streets to offer a most enthusiastic welcome.

The turnout overshadows by far Poland's recent reception given for Soviet Premier Nikita Khrushchev which seems to indicate the popular temper in what is comparatively the freest of the iron curtain countries. The demands on the Vice-President's talents in tact and diplomacy are possibly the greatest of his entire tour.

On their return to the United States, the Nixons are greeted warmly by a crowd of nearly 4,000 people including most of the White House staff as well as just about every Republican congressman and senator.

The Vice-President's remarks appear to be non-partisan: *"The people of the Soviet Union, and even more the people of Poland, who lost one out of four citizens in World War II, have suffered a great deal in wartime and they desperately want peace."*

WHAT A YEAR IT WAS!

Western Europe

IRELAND'S PRIME MINISTER EAMON DE VALERA Resigns Post In Order To Run For The Presidency.

EAMON DE VALERA ELECTED PRESIDENT OF IRELAND. Sean Lemass Takes Over As Prime Minister.

JOHN D. PROFUMO Appointed Britain's Minister Of State, Foreign Office.

TO SPUR ECONOMIC GROWTH, Britain Passes One Billion Dollar Tax Cut.

ENGLAND'S HOUSE OF COMMONS Sees Double Majority Under Macmillan's Leadership.

CHARLES DE GAULLE Is Sworn In As President Of The Fifth Republic At Inaugural Ceremony Held At The Elysee Palace In Paris And Now Wields More Power Than Any French Leader Since Emperor Napoleon III.

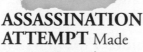

ASSASSINATION ATTEMPT Made Against France's **Francois Mitterrand.**

SPAIN BECOMES 18th MEMBER Of Organization For European Economic Cooperation.

SPECIAL ELECTORAL COLLEGE Elects **Heinrich Luebke** President Of West Germany.

PRESIDENT EISENHOWER RECEIVES WARM WELCOME By West Germans Who Yell *"We Stand By Your Side."*

Citing "Continuously Hostile Attitude" Of The 18-Member National Council, Monaco's **Prince Rainier III** Suspends The 1911 Constitution Appointing An Eight-Member Council To Help Him Administer The Principality.

Rainier III

Map labels: Norway, Sweden, Finland, Oslo, Helsinki, Stockholm, Edinburgh, Denmark, Copenhagen, United Kingdom, Berlin, Poland, Warsaw, Dublin, London, Amsterdam, Holland, Belgium, Brussels, Luxembourg, Prague, Czechoslovakia, Paris, Germany, France, Zurich, Vienna, Switzerland, Austria, Budapest, Hungary, Belgrade, Yugoslavia, Portugal, Madrid, Spain, Italy, Rome, Albania, Greece, Athens

✴ Charged With Inciting Violence, Belgian Congo's PATRICE LUMUMBA Is Arrested After Troops Fire On Mobs Rioting For Independence.

✴ Civil War Impedes Plans For Congo Independence.

✴ U. S. Troops To Leave Morocco By 1963 According To Announcement Made Jointly By PRESIDENT EISENHOWER And KING MOHAMMED.

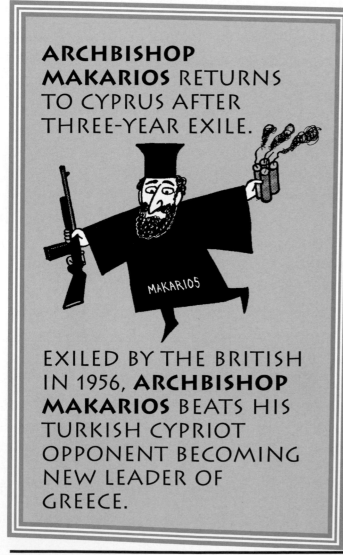

ARCHBISHOP MAKARIOS RETURNS TO CYPRUS AFTER THREE-YEAR EXILE.

MAKARIOS

EXILED BY THE BRITISH IN 1956, **ARCHBISHOP MAKARIOS** BEATS HIS TURKISH CYPRIOT OPPONENT BECOMING NEW LEADER OF GREECE.

✴ French PRESIDENT DE GAULLE To Offer Algeria Elected Government.

✴ PRESIDENT DE GAULLE'S Speech On Algerian Independence Results In Walk-Out Of Nine Gaullist Deputies.

✴ Under PRIME MINISTER HENDRIK VERVOERD'S Government, South Africa Passes A "Bantustan" Bill Removing All Coloreds From The Common Electoral Roll And Voting Age Is Reduced To 18 To Increase The Number Of White Votes Deepening Apartheid.

Middle East 1959

- Iran Accepts U. S. Proposal For Aid Rejecting Soviet Offer.

- Iran Renounces Pact Made With Soviet Union In 1921.

- Continued Aid Pledged To Iran, Pakistan And Turkey By U.S.

- Syria Reports Iraqi Air Attack.

- Following The Revolution, Iraq Pulls Out Of Baghdad Pact.

- A New Constitution Fashioned After The U. S. Constitution Is Signed By President Habib Bourguiba Of Tunisia.

- Diplomatic Relations Reopen Between Jordan And United Arab Republic.

- Central Treaty Organization (CENTO) Holds First Meeting With Baghdad Pact Ministers Under New Name.

Jordan's King Hussein Vows End Of Feud With Egypt's President Nasser.

Nasser Arrests 200 Communists.

Gamal A. Nasser

- Egypt And The Sudan End 30-Year Rivalry Agreeing To Share The Waters Of Nile River – Paves Way For Construction Of Aswan Dam.

- Iraqi Premier Kassem Wounded In Assassination Attempt.

- Shimon Peres Becomes Israel's Deputy Minister Of Defense.

- Arab League Council Warns Hungary, Poland And Rumania That Jewish Emigration To Israel Is Supporting Aggression On Arab States.

- Addressing The United Nations, Israeli Foreign Minister Golda Meir Denounces U.A.R. For Barring Israeli Ships From Suez Canal.

- Under Ben Gurion's Leadership, Israel's Mapai Party Gains In Legislative Elections.

Golda Meir   David Ben Gurion

WHAT A YEAR IT WAS!

23

NATO TO LOSE French Mediterranean Support In Case Of War.

NEWLY-FORMED International Development Association Approved By 68 World Bank Nations.

AUSTRIA, BRITAIN, DENMARK, NORWAY, PORTUGAL, SWEDEN AND SWITZERLAND, Europe's Outer Seven Nations, Form Free Trade Region.

U. N. GENERAL ASSEMBLY Adopts East-West Resolution To Establish U. N. Committee On The Peaceful Uses Of Outer Space.

FRANCE ASKED BY U.N. Not To Make Nuclear Bombs.

President Of Haiti Francois Duvalier Announces Suspension Of Dictatorial Powers.

Romulo Betancourt Sworn In As Constitutional President Of Venezuela.

U. S. Troops Called In To Quell Riots Over American Control Of Panama Canal Zone.

24

WHAT A YEAR IT WAS!

PEOPLE

Fidel Castro

receives a tumultuous welcome in New York City in one of the most enthusiastic receptions for a visiting notable in quite a while.

A cheering, singing, flag-waving crowd of thousands gather to greet the Cuban revolutionary leader and premier.

Outside Penn Station, police break up a demonstration of supporters of ousted dictator Batista.

A heavily guarded Castro makes his way past the security guards to greet the crowd despite rumors of assassination plots against him.

Almost swamped by the excited crowd, it takes Castro a record 24 minutes to cross the street to his hotel.

1959 ADVERTISEMENT

Budweiser®

Where there's Life...there's Bud®

HARMONY. Right on the label
you'll find a list of the
ingredients that blend together
to make Budweiser the masterpiece
it is...the King of Beers.

ANHEUSER-BUSCH, INC. · ST. LOUIS · NEWARK · LOS ANGELES · MIAMI

26

Quiz Show *Scandal*

In the Senate hearing room,

the dramatic climax of the probe of fixed and rigged quiz shows is taking place.

Charles' wife and father, poet Mark Van Doren, are among the spectators.

Committee chairman, Senator Orin Harris *(left)*, opens the hearing as Charles Van Doren *(right)* arrives to apologize and explain to the millions of fans whose friendship and respect he had won.

In his quiz show appearances, Van Doren won $129,000 and earned a handsome broadcasting contract. Van Doren retracts his earlier denials of getting any assistance and admits he received dramatic coaching, the questions and many of the answers.

His statement is a rueful and moving realization that for his wealth and fame he paid a bitterly high price.

1959

After a 10-year absence, **Ingrid Bergman** returns to Hollywood to host the Academy Awards ceremony.

Ingrid Bergman and her film director former husband, Roberto Rossellini, are ordered to appear in a Roman court when Rossellini refuses to return their three children to Miss Bergman after they vacationed with their dad in Italy.

Ingrid Bergman wins custody battle in Paris courtroom over her three children with Italian director Roberto Rossellini.

⭐ Actress **DIANE VARSI** Gives Up Promising Hollywood Career And Goes Into Seclusion In Bennington, Vermont Stating That Acting Is Detrimental To Her Well Being.

⭐ Suffering From Nervous Fatigue, Hollywood's Beautiful **LINDA DARNELL** Is Hypnotized To Help Her Memorize The Lines For Her Role In The Play "Late Love" Opening In Chicago And Receives Wonderful Reviews.

⭐ Spending Almost Nine Months At The Menninger Clinic Recovering From A Nervous Breakdown, Hollywood Star **GENE TIERNEY** Works As A Sales Lady In A Small Ladies Apparel Shop In Topeka, Kansas.

ELIZABETH TAYLOR CONVERTS TO JUDAISM,
THE RELIGION OF HER LATE HUSBAND, MIKE TODD AND THE RELIGION OF HER SOON-TO- BE-HUSBAND, EDDIE FISHER.

Taylor & Todd

GARY COOPER CONVERTS TO CATHOLICISM AT THE CHURCH OF THE GOOD SHEPHERD IN BEVERLY HILLS, CALIFORNIA.

TO ALEC, WITH LOVE
Having Won An Oscar For His Brilliant Performance In The Bridge On The River Kwai, **ALEC GUINNESS** Hits Queen Elizabeth's List Of Honorees Becoming A Knight Bachelor - Heretofore To Be Known As Sir Alec.

JUDITH ANDERSON Is Made British Dame

PLEASE DON'T PICK THE FLOWERS
During a party at Rio de Janeiro's Copacabana Hotel, much to the joy of the assembled press corp., **JAYNE MANSFIELD** loses the top of her dress bearing her heavily endowed 40-21-36 figure after overly enthusiastic Brazilian fans pick the strategically placed roses attached to her dress causing fall-out. Her Mr. Universe husband, Mickey Hargitay, saves the day by wrapping her in his coat.

UP WITH THE NECKLINES GIRLS!
Sex kittens **BRIGITTE BARDOT** and **KIM NOVAK** vow to give up sexy, "bitchy" parts in exchange for more serious roles.

EVERYBODY'S BABE
Much to the chagrin of new French army recruit, Jacques Charrier, when he reports to his assigned barracks, he finds a pin-up picture of his beautiful wife, **BRIGITTE BARDOT**, hanging over practically every bed.

Bardot

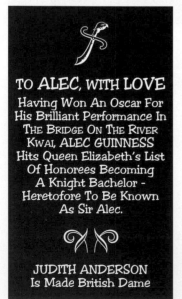

WHAT A YEAR IT WAS!

I SAID NO PICTURES PLEASE

Star of *"The World Of Suzie Wong,"* **France Nuyen** slugs it out with photographers at a Miami airport when they insist on taking pictures of her and her travelling companion, **Marlon Brando**.

Crowd and reporter shy **Ava Gardner** irritates the Australian press by refusing to show up for a scheduled press conference.

Hollywood Designer Don Loper Voices His Dissatisfaction With Princess Grace's Look Created By Paris Designers Saying That She Was More Glamourous When He Dressed Her.

They Don't Wanna Come Up And See Her Sometime

CBS Cancels Scheduled "Person To Person" Airing Of Charles Collingwood's Interview With **MAE WEST** After CBS Officials Decide The Show Is "Too Hot To Handle."

LIBERACE Is Awarded $22,500 In Damages In His Libel Suit Against The London "Daily Mirror" Over A Column Written By William Neil Connor Implying That He Is A Homosexual.

As Leading Lady GINA LOLLOBRIGIDA Looks On In Horror, Actor Luis Santana Bursts Into Flames On The Set Of King Vidor's "Solomon and Sheba" When He Brushes Against A Flaming Brazier.

Following A Year's Absence From Baseball After A Crippling Car Accident That Ended His Career, **ROY CAMPANELLA** Takes A Job As East Coast Assistant Supervisor Of Scouting For Los Angeles Dodgers As Well As Spring Training Coach At A Salary Of $25,000 A Year.

DON'T SPEND IT ALL AT ONCE, ELVIS

Elvis Presley is promoted from Private First Class to Specialist Fourth Class with a monthly pay hike from $108.37 to $135.30.

ELVIS IS ALIVE AND WELL AND STILL WEARING HIS BLUE SUEDE SHOES

Elvis Presley fans from all over the world deluge information officers in his Third Armored Division headquarters in Frankfurt, Germany after a newspaper runs a story that the singer is killed in a traffic accident.

A SAD ENDING FOR ONE WHO BROUGHT SO MUCH HAPPINESS

63-year old surviving member of the Abbott & Costello comedy team, **Bud Abbott**, doesn't have much to smile about these days. The IRS wants $500,000 in back taxes and Bud says he's broke. To make matters worse, they have forced him to put his house up for sale and Bud is wondering where have all his pals gone.

Douglas MacArthur, former supreme commander of Allied forces in the far east, celebrates his 79th birthday in New York.

The General receives a congratulatory message from pre-World War II aide, Dwight D. Eisenhower.

After a long and valiant struggle, Secretary of State **John Foster Dulles** succumbs to cancer while carrying on arduous negotiations over Berlin. His passing deeply stirs friends and foes alike throughout the world.

Despite Being Married To Kay Williams, 17 Years His Junior, Hollywood's No. 1 Matinee Idol, **CLARK GABLE**, Declares That At 58, It's Unrealistic For Him To Continue Playing A Suave Lover As The Public Disapproves Of Older Guys Chasing Leading Ladies Young Enough To Be Their Daughters.

Singer-actor SAMMY DAVIS, JR. stars in an all-Negro* western on TV's "Zane Grey Theater" in which he plays a corporal in the cavalry.

CBS hires CHARLES KURALT as a correspondent.

* Negro was the commonly used term in 1959.

WHAT A YEAR IT WAS!

Monaco's Prince Rainier and former Hollywood actress, Princess Grace, visit the Pope.

Prince Rainier and Princess Grace are accompanied by Vatican representatives as they prepare to be received by the Pope.

In a private 25-minute talk with the royal couple, the pontiff congratulates them for the influence their tiny state makes to the world of culture and art and for their devotion to the church.

WHAT A YEAR IT WAS!

SHE COULD HAVE DANCED ALL NIGHT IF SHE ONLY HAD HER SHOE

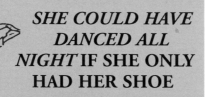

Sporting A New Hair-Do, **Princess Margaret** Goes Out For A Night On London Town And Loses Her Shoe On The Dance Floor.

Rumors Abound About A Royal Romance Between Britain's 28-Year Old **Princess Margaret** And Rome Resident 31-Year Old Prince Henry Of Hesse.

THE HIGH PRICE OF DUTY

Princess Margaret's Ex-Suitor, Former R.A.F. Group Captain Peter Townsend, Announces His Engagement To Marie-Luce Jamagne Four Years After The Princess Was Compelled To Give Him Up Because Of His Previous Marriage.

SOMEDAY HER PRINCE WILL COME
(THEY HOPE)

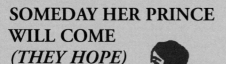

As She Celebrates Her 29th Birthday, The British Press Voices Its Concerns As To Whether Or Not **Princess Margaret** Will Ever Marry.

Prince Philip lays keel of Britain's first nuclear submarine.

A ROYAL ITCH

Prince Charles contracts chicken pox and is isolated from rest of the family over Easter break from Cheam School.

Queen Mother Elizabeth and Princess Margaret visit the Pope in a 20-minute private audience.

THE DUKE DENIES DOING THE DUNKING

Buckingham Palace releases a statement denying that the Duke Of Edinburgh had anything to do with setting off a sprinkler drenching two photographers at a Chelsea flower show.

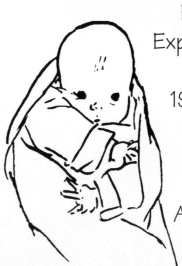

Elizabeth II Is Expecting Her Third Child In Early 1960 According To A Buckingham Palace Announcement.

WHAT A YEAR IT WAS!

Crown Prince Akihito defies 2,600-year old tradition and marries commoner, Michiko Shoda. Riding in their carriage, the royal couple is attacked by 19-year old spectator who tries to pull Michiko out by the hair. His reason: he is downcast over college entrance exams.

THE PRINCE VISITS THE IN-LAWS

Toppling yet another tradition, Crown Prince Akihito visits the home of his in-laws — becoming the first Japanese Crown Prince to do so.

TENNIS ANYONE?

Japan's Crown Princess Michiko

puts on cute little lace panties and plays a round of mixed-doubles with her husband Crown Prince Akihito.

PUTTIN' ON THE DOG

The Duke Of Windsor's Pet Pug Imperial II Wins First Prize And A Silver Cup At The International Dog Show In Deauville, France.

Britain's Queen Elizabeth II Is Fined $140 By The Jockey Club For Failing To Notify The Club Before The Champion Stakes Race That Her Horse, "Above Suspicion" Would Not Be Running.

INDIA WELCOMES THE DUKE OF EDINBURGH, FIRST MEMBER OF THE BRITISH ROYAL FAMILY TO VISIT SINCE INDIA'S INDEPENDENCE IN 1947.

28-YEAR OLD BACHELOR KING BAUDOUIN Of Belgium Makes His First State Visit Abroad To America.

CROWN PRINCE OF LAOS Is Formally Proclaimed King On The Death Of His Father King Sisavang Vong.

Princess Grace and Prince Rainier check into Rome's Grand Hotel bringing with them an entourage occupying three suites and a huge supply of their favorite champagne for a party for 500 guests.

Prince Rainier of Monaco celebrates his 36th birthday at the cabaret in Monte Carlo by playing the drums, with Her Serene Highness, Princess Grace on the tambourine and Greek shipping magnate Aristotle Onassis on the guitar.

Princess Grace is doing beautifully after her appendix is removed in Lausanne, Switzerland.

Certified winner over all

25.2% more

The Economy Champ—Ford F-100 Styleside pickup —is the smoothest riding, too! Available in 6½- or 8-foot box lengths, conventional or 4-wheel drive.

'59 FORD

It's a fact—for every 100 mile driven, Ford delivered an extr 25 gas-free miles over the aver age of other makes!

This rate of savings for For pickups was certified by th nation's foremost independen automotive research organiza tion in the greatest test of true economy ever made—Econom Showdown U.S.A.

Here's how the tests we made: First, new six-cylind half-ton pickups of the s leading makes were purchase from authorized dealers, brok

other leading pickups!

miles per gallon

in for at least 600 miles, then tuned to manufacturers' specifications.

Next, all were tested under the exact same conditions—at 30 mph, at 45 mph, at 60, in door-to-door retail delivery service, and in city driving. When the results were tabulated, there was no question of the winner...

Ford won *every* test...against *every* truck! Delivered 25.2% more miles per gallon than the average of all other makes! And that's *certified!*

25.2% more miles per gallon means getting 25 *extra* miles for every 100 miles driven! And in the course of a year's driving —say 10,000 miles—it would mean a dividend of 2,500 extra gas-free miles!

When you add this proven economy to Ford's smooth ride, extra loadspace, years of service and low price tag, you've got a combination that can't be matched. First chance, stop by your Ford Dealer's. Examine the facts and figures... the certified Economy Showdown

record. See how a '59 Ford puts you further ahead every mile you drive!

Go FORD-WARD for savings

FORD TRUCKS COST LESS

LESS TO OWN...
LESS TO RUN...
LAST LONGER, TOO!

Indian Prime Minister Nehru

gives refuge to the **Dalai Lama**, spiritual and temporal ruler of **Tibet**, along with thousands of his countrymen who were forced to flee their country after Red China stamped out rebellion in the remote mountain land making Tibet the Hungary of Asia.

In further developments, Nehru and India are further beset by Red China's claims to frontier territory leading to armed clashes along the Tibetan border.

LET MY PEOPLE GO—
The Struggle Continues

IN SECLUSION IN INDIA, Tibet's Exiled Dalai Lama, 24, Decides To Step Out To See A Showing Of "THE TEN COMMANDMENTS" Which He Very Much Enjoys.

MOUNT EVEREST CONQUEROR Sir Edmund Hillary Is Refused Entry Into Tibet By The Chinese Communist Government.

WHAT A YEAR IT WAS!

In a Cinderella story,

21-year old former maid, *Anne Marie Rasmussen* marries *Steven Rockefeller* in a tiny, unpretentious rural church in Norway.

Reporters and 5,000 well-wishers gather to witness this fairy-tale moment.

Governor and Mrs. Rockefeller (right) and Mr. & Mrs. Rasmussen gather on the steps of the church following the ceremony.

In keeping with Norwegian tradition, the couple did not kiss during the ceremony but they do so for the American cameramen.

The beaming couple wave to the crowd who wish them a happily-ever-after ending.

In a somewhat more pretentious wedding, **SHAH PAHLAVI OF IRAN** takes a third wife, marrying beautiful commoner 21-year old Farah Diba, with the hope that she will present him with a son and heir to the thousands of years old throne.

1959

Thrice Wed Zsa Zsa Gabor Returns 42 Carat Blue-White Diamond Engagement Ring To California Builder Hal Hayes Stating That She Needed To Be Swept Off Her Feet.

✦—❈—✦

Debbie Reynolds Grants Her Husband, Eddie Fisher, The Right To Get A Quickie Nevada Divorce So He Can Marry Elizabeth Taylor, Which He Does 3 1/2 Hours After The Divorce Becomes Final.

✦—❈—✦

In Court To Get His Ex-Wife To Comply With His Visitation Rights, Marlon Brando And Anna Kashfi Do Not Look At Each Other But Agree Through Their Attorneys To An Out-Of-Court Settlement.

✦—❈—✦

Jimmy "The Schnoz" Durante, 66, Unmarried Since The Death Of His Wife In 1943, Announces His Engagement To Margie Little, 38, With The Wedding To Take Place Next Year.

COUPLING

Claire Bloom & Rod Steiger
Brigitte Bardot & Jacques Charrier
Terry Moore & Stuart Cramer
Margaret O'Brien & Harold Robert Allen, Jr.
Elliott Roosevelt, Jr. & Jo Anne McFadden
Joe Louis & Martha Jefferson
Elizabeth Taylor & Eddie Fisher
Charles Coburn & Winifred Natzka
Stan Freberg & Donna Jean Andreson
George Sanders & Benita Hume Colman
Gene Krupa & Patricia Bowler
Julie Andrews & Tony Walton
Vivian Blaine & Milton R. Rackmil
Ernest Borgnine & Katy Jurado
James Coburn & Beverly Kelly
Dorothy Malone & Jacques Bergerac
Dorothy Dandridge & Jack Denison
June Lockhart & John Lindsay
Merv Griffin & Julann Wright
Victor Mature & Adrianne Joy Urwick
Sammy Davis, Jr. & Loray White

WHAT A YEAR IT WAS!

UN COUPLING

Hugh Hefner & Millie Williams
Arlene Dahl & Fernando Lamas
Esther Williams & Ben Gage
Marlon Brando & Anna Kashfi
Debbie Reynolds & Eddie Fisher
Billy Rose & Joyce Matthews
Otto Preminger & Mary Gardner Preminger
Sammy Davis, Jr. & Loray White Davis
Rod Steiger & Sally Gracie
Mickey Rooney & Elaine Mahnken
John Drew Barrymore & Cara Williams
Ernest Borgnine & Rhoda Kemins
Anita Ekberg & Anthony Steele
Betsy Drake & Cary Grant
Glenn Ford & Eleanor Powell
Deborah Kerr & Anthony Bartley
Vera Miles & Gordon Scott
Veronica Lake & Joseph A. McCarthy
Audrey Meadows & Randolph Rouse

MONEY DIDN'T BRING HER HAPPINESS
Aristotle Onassis Sued For Divorce By His Wife Of 13 Years, Tina Mary Onassis.

After A 10-Year Marriage, Diva Maria Callas, 35, And Her Husband, Giovanni Meneghini, 64, Announce Their Separation.

Heiress Gloria Vanderbilt Battles It Out In Court With Ex-Husband Leopold Stokowski Over Custody Of Their Two Children.

WHAT DO YOU THINK HE'S DOING... HAVING A PICNIC?
Separated From His Third Wife, Betsy, Hollywood Hunk Cary Grant Attends The Grand Finale Of The Cannes Film Festival With Beautiful Kim Novak Where They Danced, Danced, Danced, All Night.

On his state visit to the U. S., Soviet Premier Nikita Khrushchev gets to see the filming of "Can Can" and meets Shirley MacLaine, Frank Sinatra, Maurice Chevalier and Louis Jourdan. Citing security reasons, however, and much to his chagrin, the Soviet leader is barred from Disneyland.

★ New England Poet **Robert Frost,** Four-Time Pulitzer Prize Winner, Celebrates His 85th Birthday Predicting That Senator Jack Kennedy Will Be The Next President Of The United States.

★ Poet **Carl Sandburg** Mesmerizes A Joint Session Of Congress As He Expounds On The 150th Birthday Of Abraham Lincoln.

CHURCHILL

Despite Warnings From His Doctor, Winston Churchill Schedules U. S. Trip To Visit With President Eisenhower.

HOW LOW CAN YOU GET?

Thieves make off with Lady Churchill's jewelry and furs and if that isn't bad enough, they also steal three boxes of the former prime minister's favorite cigars.

Winston Churchill Wins Seat In Parliament Making Him One Of The Oldest Members.

Sir Winston Churchill Celebrates His 85th Birthday Surrounded By His Ten Grandchildren, Champagne And A Cake Containing One Candle For Each Year.

Sir Winston Churchill's Daughter, Sarah, Is Arrested In London For Public Drunkenness And Fined $5.60.

THE WHITE HOUSE REVISITED

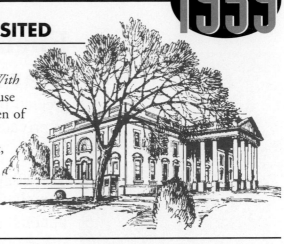

Celebrating their 40th anniversary, the Women's National Press Club gives a *"Life With Father"* luncheon and tour of the White House with Mamie Eisenhower, inviting the children of presidents including Major John Eisenhower, John Coolidge, James Roosevelt, Richard Cleveland, Mrs. Alice Roosevelt Longworth, Mrs. Helen Taft Manning, Mrs. Marion Cleveland Amen and Mrs. Eleanor Wilson McAdoo.

IS YOUTH WASTED ON THE OLD?

A Gallop Poll shows presidential hopeful Democratic Senator **John Kennedy** would be defeated by New York Governor Nelson Rockefeller. The young Senator receives other discouraging news slipping behind Adlai Stevenson in New Jersey as voters voice their concern that Kennedy is too young to lead our Allied leaders who range in age from 60's (Harold Macmillan, Charles de Gaulle) to 80's (Konrad Adenauer).

An early Gallop Poll indicates that **Richard Nixon** could easily defeat Senator John Kennedy or Adlai Stevenson.

President Eisenhower gives presidential hopeful Democratic Senator John Kennedy's campaign a boost saying that he didn't know if a Catholic could be elected president but that a candidate should not be barred simply because he is Catholic.

Governor Rockefeller withdraws as a 1960 presidential candidate.

Mrs. Eleanor Roosevelt Guest Of Honor At London Luncheon, Along With Her Granddaugher Nina, Attended By Lady Churchill And Former Prime Minister Clement Attlee To Launch The British Edition Of Her Autobiography.

21-Year Old Granddaughter Of Nationalist Chinese President Chiang Kai-shek Quietly Enrolls At Mills College In Oakland, California.

New York Governor Rockefeller's Norwegian Daughter-in-Law Anne Marie Enrolls In Columbia University For An Intermediate English Course For Foreigners.

OH PLEASE GRANDMA, I'D WALK A MILE FOR THIS ONE

Visiting A Bazaar In Beersheba, Israel With Her Famous Grandmother, **Mrs. Eleanor Roosevelt**, 16-Year Old Nina Falls In Love With A Baby Camel Whom She Names "Duchess" And Implores Her Granny To Buy it For Her, Which She Does For $77.00.

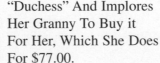

England's peppery Field Marshall Montgomery is warmly greeted by Soviet Premier Nikita Khrushchev for two days of private talks on a wide range of world affairs.

Montgomery's unofficial visit is viewed with loud apprehension by the British press as earlier he had announced that American leadership of the free world has deteriorated.

Montgomery recants and gives a mild apology for belittling American leadership and says he is optimistic that war over Berlin can be avoided.

IN A RADIO AND TELEVISION SPEECH To The Nation, President Eisenhower Reports That Wherever He Went On His 11-Nation Tour He Found A Deep Longing For Peace.

SON OF THE ARMY'S First Negro General Officer, Air Force Brigadier General Benjamin Oliver Davis, Jr. Is Nominated By President Eisenhower For Promotion To Two-Star Rank Which Would Make Him The Highest-Ranking Negro In U. S. Armed Forces History.

JIMMY STEWART AWARDED RANK Of Brigadier General By The Senate Armed Services Committee Ending An Air Force Two-Year Battle With Senator Margaret Chase Smith Who Had Been Blocking The Promotion.

U. S. ADMIRAL R. L. Dennison Is Appointed Supreme Allied Commander In The Atlantic.

THE U. S. SENATE CONFIRMS The Appointment Of Ogden R. Reid As U.S. Ambassador To Israel.

POPE JOHN XXIII Appeals To World Leaders To Work For Unity And Peace In His First Encyclical.

WHAT A YEAR IT WAS!

No other Jet to Europe offers you the extra comfort of Pan Am's exclusive first-class lounge.

Halfway to Europe between cocktails and coffee

Don't plan to catch up on your reading. There's too much to take in—too much to talk about on your first Jet Clipper* flight.

While the stewardess removes the last cordial glass from your dinner table, she reminds you to set your watch five hours ahead and tells you that there's barely enough time to finish a chapter before you see the lights of London.

Pan Am Jets are fastest to London, the only Jets to Paris and Rome. And this summer, Pan Am is increasing its schedules to include as many as four Jet flights a day to Europe—with deluxe *President Special* service available on every one. You can also fly economy-class Clipper Thrift service, if you wish, with fares starting as low as $453.60† round trip.

For reservations, call your Travel Agent or any of Pan Am's 61 offices in the U. S. and Canada.

*Trade-Mark. Reg. U. S. Pat. Off.   †Fares subject to change.

World's Most Experienced Airline

Pan Am Jet Clippers...world's fastest airliners...the only economy-class Jet service... the only Jets to all three capitals: London, Paris and Rome.

43

NOW WHAT EXACTLY IS IT THAT YOU DO FOR A LIVING?

Claiming he was in real estate at the time of his naturalization swearing-in when in fact he was a bootlegger, FRANK COSTELLO loses his U. S. citizenship paving the way for his deportation back to Italy.

JAILED FOR GIVING THE SOVIETS A-BOMB SECRETS, DR. KLAUS EMIL FUCHS IS RELEASED FROM A LONDON JAIL.

England's Prima Ballerina Dame Margot Fonteyn is arrested in Panama on the grounds that her husband, Roberto Arias, is involved in a suspected revolutionary plot.

OY VEY BLUES

AMERICA'S AMBASSADOR OF JAZZ, LOUIS ARMSTRONG, IS ACCUSED OF BEING A SPY BY THE EGYPTIAN NEWSPAPER, AL AHRAM, CHARGING THAT HE RAN AN ISRAELI SPY RING CONSISTING OF SINGERS AND DANCERS.

21 Top Mafia Racketeers

Including **Joseph Profaci, John C. Montana** And **Vito Genovese** Are Rounded Up In Huge Crackdown By Federal Narcotic Agents In A Sweep Extending From New York To California Charging Them With Conspiring To Obstruct Justice.

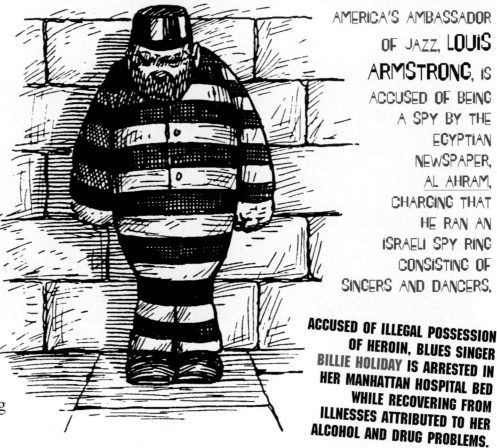

ACCUSED OF ILLEGAL POSSESSION OF HEROIN, BLUES SINGER BILLIE HOLIDAY IS ARRESTED IN HER MANHATTAN HOSPITAL BED WHILE RECOVERING FROM ILLNESSES ATTRIBUTED TO HER ALCOHOL AND DRUG PROBLEMS.

GETTING CRIME TO PAY

"Reformed" Gangster MICKEY COHEN Gets Hollywood Agent To Book Him On The Lecture Circuit To Give Talks On Why Crime Doesn't Pay For Fees Ranging From $1,000 To $2,500.

WHO YOU CALLING A DEADBEAT DAD?

A patient at New York's Presbyterian Hospital for treatment of an injured knee, swashbuckler ERROL FLYNN is served with a subpoena from his former wife while getting his whirlpool treatment. Her gripe? Errol is not sending child support.

WHO YOU CALLING A BABALOO?

Television producer and co-star of "I Love Lucy," DESI ARNAZ is arrested in Hollywood for being drunk and has to post $21 in bail which he forfeits when he does not show up in court.

WHAT A YEAR IT WAS!

Texas-born winner of Moscow's Tchaikovsky Festival last year, 24-year old **Van Cliburn** undergoes surgery on the infected middle finger of his right hand and after seven weeks is able to resume limited daily practice.

French chanteuse, **Edith Piaf**, is recovering from the removal of a peptic ulcer after surgery in New York.

BEING IN THE MOMENT

In his pursuit of realism, while shooting "One-Eyed Jacks," method actor **Marlon Brando** winds up with a cut over his right eye requiring stitches.

WHAT ABOUT A GAME OF DARTS INSTEAD?

Robert Mitchum shows up on the set of "A Terrible Beauty" with a black eye and an assortment of cuts and bruises sustained in a drunken brawl at a Dublin pub the night before.

♦ **BESS TRUMAN**, 74-year old wife of former president Harry S. Truman, undergoes surgery for the removal of a benign breast tumor in a Kansas City hospital while daughter Margaret Truman Daniel gives birth through a cesarean section to a 7 lb. 3 oz. boy at New York's Doctor's Hospital.

♦ **HAVING SUFFERED TWO MISCARRIAGES**, actress **Marilyn Monroe**, 33, checks into Manhattan hospital for gynecological surgery which she hopes will enable her to have a baby.

♦ **LOUIS "SATCHMO" ARMSTRONG** takes ill in Italy suffering from pneumonia brought on by emphysema.

♦ **MAMIE EISENHOWER** checks into Maine Chance, a weight control spa in Arizona.

♦ **AN EMOTIONAL** radio and television entertainer **Arthur Godfrey** checks out of Manhattan's Columbia-Presbyterian Medical Center after the removal of a malignant tumor from his lung.

♦ **VIOLET-EYED BEAUTY Elizabeth Taylor**, 27, is hospitalized with viral pneumonia while golden-throat **Judy Garland**, 37, is hospitalized with hepatitis.

♦ **IRA GERSHWIN**, 62, undergoes stomach surgery for the second time in 18 months.

♦ **AUDREY HEPBURN** suffers two fractured vertebrae in her back when thrown from a horse during the filming of "The Unforgiven."

♦ **HEART ATTACK SURVIVOR President Eisenhower** honors fellow heart attack survivor Senate majority leader, **Lyndon B. Johnson** with the annual Heart Association's award for "meeting the personal challenges of heart disease."

♦ **COMEDIAN JONATHAN WINTERS**, 33, is hospitalized in San Francisco after suffering a nervous breakdown.

♦ **61-YEAR OLD** Nobel Prize winning writer, **William Faulkner**, suffers a broken collar bone when he falls from his horse during a jump at the Farmington Hunt Club near Charlottesville, Virginia.

♦ **DOCTORS DISCOVER** blood clot behind **Bob Hope's** left eye during the filming of a television show in Hollywood and order the 54-year old comedian to rest or run the risk of losing his eye.

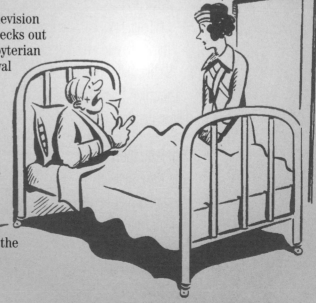

45

1959

ERNEST HEMINGWAY

Celebrates His 60th Birthday In Spain By Going To A Bullfight.

After Nearly 1,500 Performances In New York And London As Eliza Doolittle, "My Fair Lady's" Julie Andrews Sings To Professor Higgins For The Last Time.

Prima Donna Maria Callas receives a dozen curtain calls after her peformance in "Medea" in London's Covent Garden. All performances are sold out with the most expensive seats ordinarily selling for $11.76 being scalped at $70.

Banned from the Metropolitan Opera, Maria Callas performs brilliantly in concert at Carnegie Hall under the auspices of the American Opera Society with ticket prices as high as $33 per ticket.

Painter **Pablo Picasso** donates two paintings for Paris auction to benefit flood victims in the French Riviera town of Frejus and urges other artists to make similar contributions.

81-year old cellist **Pablo Casals** declares "rock 'n' roll a disease that will pass away as quickly as it was created."

MARLENE DIETRICH

Makes Her Singing Debut At Paris' Etoile Theatre With Jean Cocteau, Lena Horne, Orson Welles And Maurice Chevalier There To Cheer Her On.

Marlene Dietrich, The Most Glamourous Grandmother In The World, Faints As Argentine Fans Mob Her To Show Their Affection.

* 20-Year Old Cigar-Smoking **Shelagh Delaney** Hailed As Britain's Answer To Francoise Sagan On The Opening Of Her Play "A Taste Of Honey," Which Is Quickly Picked Up By American Producer David Merrick For A Broadway Debut.

* Nobel Prize Winning Author Of "Dr. Zhivago," Russian Poet-Novelist **Boris Pasternak** Attends A Performance Of The New York Philharmonic Conducted By **Leonard Bernstein** And Lavishes Great Praise On Mr. Bernstein.

* Michigan Supreme Court Justice **John D. Voelker** Turns In His Bench For A Typewriter Having Earned $500,000 For "Anatomy Of A Murder," Written Under His Pen Name Robert Travers.

* American Primitive Painter **Grandma Moses** Celebrates Her 99th Birthday.

WHAT A YEAR IT WAS!

TAKE A SHOT AND WE'LL CALL YOU IN TWO DAYS

When immigration officials discover his smallpox vaccination has expired, "Auntie Mame" author **Patrick Dennis** is denied re-entry into the United States and detained for 48 hours on returning from a 6-week tour of Russia.

✱ Contralto **Marian Anderson** Becomes First Negro Member Of Manhattan's Elite Cosmopolitan Club For Women.

✱ **Kristoffer Kristofferson**, Brilliant 22-Year Old Rhodes Scholar From Pomona College In Southern California, Answers Ad In London's "Daily Mirror" For Young Musicians And Winds Up With A Recording Contract With J. Arthur Rank's Top Rank Records And Is Renamed Kris Carson.

PUTTING ON THE DOG COWARD STYLE

Rather Than Put Them In An English Kennel, **Noel Coward** Sends His Two Poodles To A Swiss Boarding School Where They Will Be Instructed In Good Manners And How To Behave Like Gentlemen.

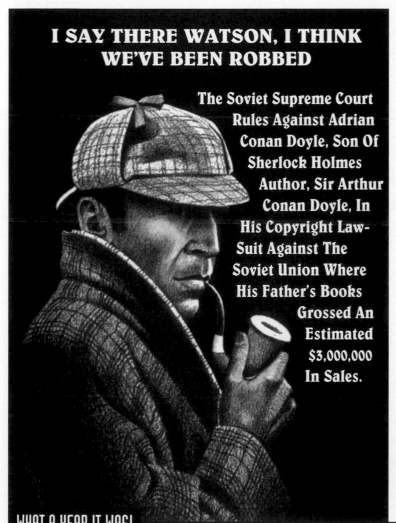

I SAY THERE WATSON, I THINK WE'VE BEEN ROBBED

The Soviet Supreme Court Rules Against Adrian Conan Doyle, Son Of Sherlock Holmes Author, Sir Arthur Conan Doyle, In His Copyright Law-Suit Against The Soviet Union Where His Father's Books Grossed An Estimated $3,000,000 In Sales.

Robert Anderson, Herbert Hoover, Marian Anderson, James R. Killian And **Frank Pace, Jr.**, Receive National Institute Of Social Sciences Gold Medals.

President Eisenhower Awards The Medal Of Freedom To **John Foster Dulles**, The Highest U.S. Civilian Award.

Bandleader Benny Goodman Presents The N.A.A.C.P.'s Spingarn Award For Highest Achievement By An American Negro To Jazz Great **Duke Ellington**.

The National Institute Of Social Science Presents Its 1959 Gold Medals For Distinguished Service To Humanity To **Dr. Jonas Salk** (Polio Vaccine,) **Helen Hayes** (Actress) And **Laurance Rockefeller** (Financier.)

Violin Virtuoso **Jascha Heifetz**, 58, Becomes Full Professor Of Music At The University Of California At Los Angeles.

SOMETHING TO BEAT THE DRUMS ABOUT

Nobel Prize winner 84-year old **Albert Schweitzer** goes to Copenhagen to receive a Sonning Prize, the Danish equivalent of the Nobel Prize, which brings with it a cash award of $14,250 which the missionary-physician will use for his famous jungle hospital in Gabon, Africa.

The Sole Survivor Of The Family That Lived In Mortal Fear Of Being Discovered In Hidden Quarters Of A House In Amsterdam, Concentration Camp Survivor **Otto Frank** And His Second Wife, Elfriede, Tour New York After Attending A Special Showing Of **"The Diary Of Anne Frank,"** A Film Based On The Diary Of His Young Daughter. Mr. Frank Plans To Establish A Youth Center In Anne's Memory In The Same Building Where The Family Hid From The Nazis.

HOW MUCH DO YOU THINK WE'LL GET FOR PARK PLACE?

A New York judge rules that four of the children of Boston millionaire **Joseph P. Kennedy** are entitled to a fair price for one of their buildings which was condemned to make room for New York City's new Lincoln Center and so **Mrs. Jean K. Smith**, **Mrs. Peter Lawford**, **Mrs. Eunice Shriver** and **Robert Kennedy** get to divvy up $2.4 million, which is the amount the judge awarded them for the property.

HENRY AND ANNE FORD Spend An Estimated $100,000 On Their Daughter Charlotte's Coming Out Party Attended By Anyone Who's Anyone From The United States And Europe.

22-Year Old **Karim Aga Khan IV** Receives His BA From Harvard University And The University Receives $50,000 From Aga Khan For Scholarships To Middle Eastern Students.

Evangelist Billy Graham spends five months preaching in Australia and New Zealand despite problems with one of his eyes.

FIRST FEMALE PRESIDENT OF THE FEDERAL AERONAUTIQUE INTERNATIONALE, U. S. AVIATRIX JACQUELINE COCHRAN, PRESIDES OVER FIRST MEETING OF THIS ORGANIZATION EVER HELD IN THE SOVIET UNION.

SOMETHING TO MAKE A BIG RACKET ABOUT

Ralph **Bunche**, Nobel Peace Prize winner and present United Nations Undersecretary for Special Political Affairs, intercedes unsuccessfully on behalf of his 15-year old son, Ralph, when he is refused membership in New York's West Side Tennis Club in Forest Hills. The club's president, Wilfred Burglund, said Forest Hills does not allow Negroes or Jews to join this prestigious club.

Public outrage is vociferous, U. S. senators issue a public statement condemning the racist practices of the West Side Tennis Club and faced with an investigation by the New York Commission on Interfaith Relations, the club's president resigns and a new policy is passed that accepts membership without regard to race, creed or color.

WHAT A YEAR IT WAS!

BEAUTY CONTEST

WINNERS

MISS AMERICA 1959
Mary Ann Mobley, 21, Brandon, Mississippi.

Tokyo's **Akiko Kojima** becomes first Asian to win the **MISS UNIVERSE** title while New York model, 20-year old **Cecilia Cooper**, becomes first Negro to win France's annual Cannes Film Festival's **MISS FESTIVAL** title.

MRS. AMERICA
Mrs. Margaret Priebe, Des Moines, Iowa.

18-year old secretarial student **Pat Williams** becomes first Negro to win the **Miss Sacramento** title.

Indiana University sophomore **Nancy Street** has a lot to smile about as she becomes the first Negro to become a beauty queen on that campus.

WHAT A YEAR IT WAS!

1959

Sigma Chi member **Warren Beatty** graduates Northwestern University.

Timothy Leary joins the faculty of Harvard University.

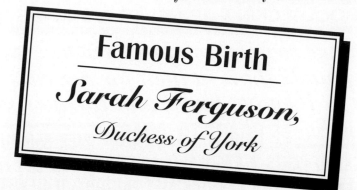

Famous Birth
Sarah Ferguson, Duchess of York

PASSINGS

Lead defense attorney in the famous Scopes "monkey" trial, **John R. Neal**, age 83, dies in Tennessee.

Joseph Barbara, in whose Apalachin, New York home the infamous meeting of dozens of underworld members took place, dies at 53 of a heart attack.

1959 ADVERTISEMENT

LA NOUVELLE GÉOGRAPHIE DE L'AUTOMOBILE
or, how to make your driving fun again: LA VILLE. The car for city living. Only 155 inches to park and maneuver. Smart, designed-in-Paris lines. Elegant, made-in-France touches. He-and-she glove compartments; sophisticated sliding sun-roof (optional extra). LES SUBURBS: COMPACT. YET ROOMY. FOUR DOORS. BIG 7 CU. FT. TRUNK UP FRONT. IDEAL FOR GROCERY-ING. TRAIN-ING. SCHOOL-PICKING-UP. NEVER A SNOW-STALL. *La Province:* Long-range seating comfort (owners report less driving fatigue on long hauls than in their former cars). Long-range economy, too. Up to 40 mpg. Fewer and cheaper maintenance bills. High resale value. LE COAST-TO-COAST: OVER 850 AUTHORIZED RENAULT DEALERS WITH FULL STOCKS OF PARTS - A REGULARLY SCHEDULED AIR-LIFT FROM FRANCE KEEPS STOCKS FULL! FACTORY-TRAINED [AND PERIODICALLY, FACTORY-REVIEWED] MECHANICS AT EACH DEALER'S. [IN CANADA, OVER 150 DEALERS.] STOP IN AT THE NEAREST RENAULT DEALER AND SEE HOW MUCH FUN IS WAITING FOR YOU. *Le P.O.E., New York:* where suggested price is $1645.* Not too much more in other places.

Le Car Hot: **RENAULT** Dauphine

*STATE AND LOCAL TAXES EXTRA. FOR ILLUSTRATED BROCHURE SEE NEAREST DEALER OR WRITE RENAULT, INC., 750 THIRD AVENUE, N.Y. 17, N.Y.   ALSO ON OVERSEAS DELIVERY PLAN.

50

HUMAN INTEREST  1959

Usually blase Londoners can't help but stare with amusement at this **space-age smog mask.**

The inventor says it is very practical and that all social amenities can be observed such as **kissing**

and **eating and drinking.**

Reader's Digest remains No. 1 in circulation followed by **LIFE**, **LOOK** and the *Saturday Evening Post*.

New York Herald Tribune columnist, Marie Torre, is thrown in jail for 10 days for contempt of court after she refuses to testify which would have compelled her to reveal confidential information.

YESTERDAY'S NEWSPAPER TODAY

Asserting that the quality of running and printing on wastepaper is the same as "new paper," the **Chicago Sun-Times** announces the use of 10,000 tons of wastepaper in its daily editions.

"Lady Chatterley's Lover" is banned from the U.S. mails on grounds the book is obscene.

Upholding first amendment rights in the case involving **"Lady Chatterley's Lover,"** New York court rules that New York cannot constitution-ally prevent the exhibition of a motion picture because the content might be contrary to popular moral, religious or legal standards.

The Clutter Family Of Holcomb, Kansas Are Found Brutally Murdered In Their Home.

- A Special Task Force Created By New York's Police Commissioner To Fight Upsurge In Youthful Offenders.

- - - - - - - - -

- The Latest FBI Reports Reveal That Los Angeles Has More Crime Than Chicago Or New York.

- - - - - - - - -

- Fort Lauderdale, Florida Beefs Up Its Police Force And Sets Up A Police Station Right On The Beach In Anticipation Of College Spring Break.

HEY LET'S TEACH KIDS NON-VIOLENCE BY PADDLING THEM IN OUR SCHOOLS

Much To The Frustration Of The Mothers Who Demand A Warrant, Memphis Sessions Judge Willard Dixon Refuses To Issue Warrant For The Arrest Of John Barnes, Principal Of Bartlett High Who Paddled 14 Children.

MEANWHILE, BACK IN CIVILIZATION...

New York's Governor Nelson Rockefeller Vetoes "Hickory Stick" Bill Pushed Through The State Assembly Authorizing Paddling Of Students As A Means Of Punishment.

the doublemint twins make their television debut.

- Dan Enright, One-Time Producer Of Six Television Quiz Shows, Including "Tic Tac Dough," "Dotto" And "Name That Tune," Testifies Before Congress That In Order To Increase Ratings, Quiz Shows Have Been Rigged For Years Down To Rehearsed Emotions And Advance Answers To Questions.

- FCC Issues Equal Time Ruling Requiring TV To Give A Forum To All Political Candidates.

- A Los Angeles Judge Grants A Divorce To A Hollywood Actress On The Grounds That Her Husband Watches Too Much Television.

New Flowers That Bloom In The Spring

PRAIRIE DAWN: Pink double blossoms, no fragrance, very hardy and will thrive on prairies.

STARFIRE: Large double medium, moderate fragrance, red flowers that bloom in candelabra-like clusters.

GOLDEN GIRL: Golden yellow double flowers, moderate fragrance, light green foliage.

GARDEN PARTY: Pale yellow double blooms with slight fragrance.

400 American schools will offer Russian in their curriculum.

Massachusetts Superior Court Judge Jennie Loitman Barren is named Mother of the Year by the American Mothers Committee.

Philosopher Hannah Arendt writes essay advocating same-sex marriage.

THEY'LL BE DANCIN', DANCIN' IN THE STREETS

10,000 Out Of The Estimated 1,000,000 Square Dancers In The U.S. Converge On Denver For The Eighth Annual National Convention Of Square Dancers.

New Dance Crazes - The Dog, The Shag And The Alligator Are Banned As Being Too Provocative.

HOT DANCES

Cha-Cha   Mambo

American Teenagers Are Less Interested In Rock 'n' Roll Dancing But Their Japanese Counterparts Are Real Enthusiasts.

The Newest of Everything Great! — *The Greatest of Everything New!*

Design you out ? No, Never !

Comfort stages a comeback. You get it in oversize doors, unobstructed entrance space, deeper seat cushioning, greater headroom. As an extra note of grace, add Dodge's new Swing-Out swivel seats.*

Now, it's nice to ride low and snug-to-the-road. You are more secure. The car is in better command.

But here's something important to you. When Dodge pioneered the low Swept-Wing car, you were designed *into* it, not *out* of it.

We figured that *solid comfort* for driver and passengers is something you're entitled to *along with lowness and beauty and style.*

The way you *get* in it, the way you *sit* in it, sets this '59 Dodge apart from the field.

We're talking about *more* than the new Swing-Out swivel seats*. We mean the size of the door opening and the clearance for your head and shoulders and knees and feet when you enter.

We mean the support under your legs, the deep cushioning at your back, the position of your body when you settle down.

This '59 Dodge was built around *you*. That is one mark of a great car. Compare it!

*optional at extra cost

'59 DODGE

Dodge brings you Lawrence Welk on television every week, ABC-TV network. Ask your Dodge dealer for time and channel.

54

Chicago's *61st Annual* Automobile Show

1959

Showcases A Glittering Array Of Vehicular Innovations

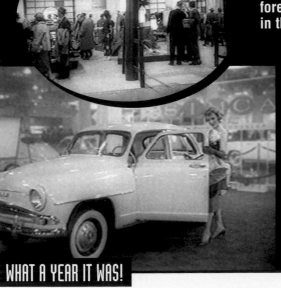

Everything you'll see on the highway in the months ahead is shown including this swivel seat *(left)* and a handy headrest for those long Sunday drives *(right).*

There's a new Japanese addition to the ranks of the little foreign cars which are becoming increasingly more popular in the U.S.

This particular model has a folding bed inside.

WHAT A YEAR IT WAS!

The First Urban Monorail System In The United States Commences Operation In Tomorrowland.

Reaching $2.5 Million In Construction Costs, The SUBMARINE VOYAGE Attraction Is Open For Business.

Disneyland Launches Its E Ticket.

Matterhorn Mountain Opens For Bobsled Business.

Disneyland News

The 15th Million Person Enters Disneyland.

PRESIDENT EISENHOWER GIVES NEW YORK APPROVAL FOR 1964 NEW YORK WORLD'S FAIR IN FLUSHING MEADOW, CHOOSING NEW YORK OVER WASHINGTON AND LOS ANGELES.

THE CITY COMES TO AN ELECTRICAL STANDSTILL AS MANHATTAN LOSES ITS POWER DURING A SWELTERING HEAT WAVE.

PUMPERNICKEL, PUMPERNICKEL, MY WEEKEND IN THE CATSKILLS FOR A PUMPERNICKEL

NEW YORK'S EBINGER BAKERY CHAIN GOES ON STRIKE AND NEW YORKERS MUDDLE THROUGH YET ANOTHER CRISIS ~ BEING DEPRIVED OF THEIR PUMPERNICKEL OR THEIR JEWISH RYE BREAD. OY.

WHO DID YOU SAY IS BURIED THERE?

NEW YORK'S GRANT'S TOMB BECOMES A NATIONAL SHRINE.

- **New York Has The Largest Population In The Country Followed By Chicago And Los Angeles.**

- **Plans Are In The Works For A Three-Stage Rapid-Transit System Including A Subway Under The Bay Between San Francisco And Oakland.**

- **Pittsburgh Celebrates Its Bicentennial With A Major Effort In Rebuilding The City.**

- **Farmers Market In Los Angeles Is #2 Tourist Attraction With Disneyland Holding The #1 Spot.**

BRIDGING THE GAPS

TIME FOR TIME SHARES

The Smith Point Bridge, first bridge linking the mainland and Fire Island on Long Island, New York is completed.

OO, LA, LA

The Tancarville, longest suspension bridge in Europe, spanning the Seine River near Le Havre, France, opens for its first crossings.

Ground is broken in New York for the $320 million Verrazano Narrows Bridge.

Construction begins on the lower deck of the George Washington Bridge.

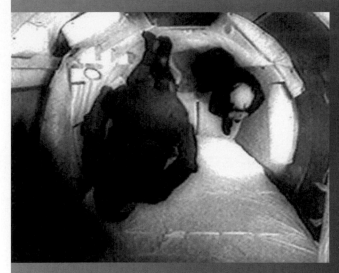

In preparation for man's first space voyage,

seven astronauts of Project Mercury, spacemen of tomorrow, experience the eerie sensation of total weightlessness in special training flights.

First Round-The-World Jet Passenger Service Is Kicked-Off By Pan-American Airways.

Construction Begins On The New Jet Airport At Chantilly, Virginia To Be Named Dulles International Airport.

FAA Rules Commercial Pilots Must Turn In Their Wings At Age 60.

The U. S. Air Force Academy In Colorado Springs, Colorado Graduates Its First Class.

France's Only Woman Test Pilot, Jacqueline Auriol Breaks Her Own World Air Speed Record Flying 1,344 m.p.h. At 37,000 Feet, Almost Double Her Former Speed.

BY THE SKIN OF HER MAST

With less than seven foot clearance, the INDEPENDENCE, world's largest aircraft carrier, barely makes it under the Brooklyn Bridge as she sets out for her first sea trial.

UNSAFE AT LOWER SPEEDS

The Lowest Accident Rate Occurs At 65 M.P.H. With Three Times As Many Accidents At 35 M.P.H.

Contrary To Popular Opinion, Women Are Not The Worst Drivers But Military Personnel Are With Five Times As Many Accidents As Civilians.

Laws Preventing School Integration Are Struck Down By Virginia Supreme Court And Segregated Schools In Arlington And Norfolk See Their First Negro Students.

Georgia Is Directed by federal courts to end segregation of its public schools.

Florida admits several Negroes to Miami's Dade County all-white schools.

FOLLY of FAUBUS

Governor Orval E. Faubus closes high schools in Little Rock, Arkansas in protest over federal court desegregation rulings.

U. S. Supreme Court overturns Arkansas law which allowed Governor Orval Faubus to close public high schools.

The riot squad is called out as a violent mob tries to prevent integration of Central High in Little Rock, Arkansas.

Local police enforce order as five Negro children enroll in Little Rock public schools after Governor Faubus accedes to federal court ruling.

Arlington And Norfolk Virginia desegregate public schools without violence.

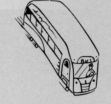

ATLANTA BUSES AND TROLLEYS are desegregated without violence.

WITH REGISTERED VOTERS BEING WHITE ONLY in a county that is 50% Negro, a Mississippi circuit appeals court ruling to overturn the murder conviction of a Negro is upheld by the Supreme Court.

FEDERAL REGISTRARS TO OVERSEE VOTING in the south requested by Civil Rights Commission.

U. S. SUPREME COURT overturns Louisiana's ban on boxing matches between whites and Negroes.

FOUR YOUNG WHITE MEN are tried and convicted of raping a Negro girl and are sentenced to life imprisonment.

AT A CONVENTION IN NEW YORK celebrating the N.A.A.C.P.'s 50th anniversary executive secretary Roy Wilkins cites the achievements of the organization including the end of lynchings and the breaking down of color barriers.

WHAT A YEAR IT WAS!

Mother Elizabeth Seton (1774-1821)

Mother Elizabeth Anne Seton first American to be beatified by the Catholic church.

EVANGELICAL LUTHERANS
and United Evangelical Lutherans join forces forming the American Lutheran Church.

ACCORDING TO THE UNITED COUNCIL OF CHURCHES, 64% of Americans belong to a church.

GIVE ME THAT OLD TIME ROCK 'N' ROLL

The congregation of Rev. Geoffrey Beaumont drinks beer and dances to rock 'n' roll hymns in his St. George's Anglican Church in London.

NO REDS IN THE ROSARY
The Pope decrees Catholics may not support the Communist party.

GET THEE TO A CHURCH
B-3 I-4 N-27 G-7 O-6. BINGO IS LEGALIZED IN NEW YORK.

COME ON FELLAS, SUCK IN THOSE TUMMIES

TELEPHONE

In keeping with the national fad, 22 students of St. Mary's College in Moraga, California sardine themselves into a telephone booth but fail to break the record of 25 established in the Union of South Africa.

THE CITY DOESN'T WANT TO GET TRIPPED UP

Mobile, Alabama passes an ordinance requiring women to obtain a high-heel license which absolves the city from damages.

IT ISN'T RAINING RAIN YOU KNOW, IT'S RAINING ROCKS

A hailstorm strikes Oklahoma dropping stones more than 10 inches in diameter.

Lava is catapulted 200 feet into the air as Kilauea Ike crater erupts.

CRAMMING CALIFORNIA STYLE

Having run out of loose change, students at California's Long Beach State College decide to switch from cramming into phone booths to trying their luck at cars and some 40 of them pile in (and out of) a Volkswagen.

WHAT A YEAR IT WAS!

59

NEW WORDS &

AMBUCOPTER
A helicopter utilized as an ambulance.

DECOUPLING
A way to conceal a nuclear blast.

ELECTRONIC FENCE
When planes and other carriers make an imaginary fence.

BEER-B-QUE
A barbecue that has beer as its prime refreshment.

DENUCLEARIZATION ZONE
An area where nuclear tests will be prohibited.

FALL-IN
Radioactive waste from peaceful purposes.

BUDGET BUSTER

An individual who spends more money than they have.

DE-SMOGGING
To eliminate smog-generating particles from automobile exhaust.

GO-KARTING
Go-kart racing.

HALF-JAIL
Where an alcoholic lives in the evening, but is allowed to leave for work.

COLD SLEEP
Hypothermia.

DISCOMFORT INDEX
A way of measuring a person's discomfort due to weather conditions.

HOT ISSUE
Stocks that will increase in price when publicly sold.

COMPUTERESE
Codes observed by a computer to decipher problems.

DUBBIDOBBER
A section of the X-15 rocket's ejection seat.

HULA HOOP DISEASE
Neck and abdominal pain found in hula hoop users.

COSMIC ROCKET
A rocket that forever leaves the earth's gravitational pull.

EVANGELIZE
To proselytize.

JETWALK
A walkway that takes passengers from the terminal to the airplane.

EXPRESSIONS

JUNGLE MARKET
When the rules of the jungle dominate business.

OUT-PRICE
To offer lower prices.

PLANETEER
One who voyages in space.

MECHTA
The name of the first Russian rocket to reach solar orbit.

PADDLE WHEEL SATELLITE
Nickname for the Explorer VI.

REVERSE PROGRAMMING
To reschedule a program at a different time than similar programming.

MICRO-SLEEP
Short relaxation periods during the day.

SALES KIT
The procedure of entertaining a potential client.

MOON HOUSE
A home for human moon dwellers.

PAGODA
A new architectural home style.

SLALOM
A type of water ski.

SOCIAL HANGOVER
The self-conscious feeling one has the day after a wild party.

NYMPHETITIS
Fear of advanced sexual displays.

PAPERIZE
To add to office procedures.

THINK CONTRACT
A contract focusing on theoretical labor.

OPEN CURTAIN
Business transactions with Russians.

VALET PARKING
When an attendant parks and retrieves a patron's automobile.

WONNY
A veteran of World War I.

Fun Flavor you can pour! There's a very special goodness to beer or ale brewed with Barley Malt. It's a bright and cheerful pleasure . . . the relaxing-with-friends kind of pleasure. *Easy pleasure!*

The goodness of Malt
adds a premium to pleasure

Barley and Malt
I N S T I T U T E

whose members are U.S. malting companies that guide sun-ripened barley through a natural process with scientific care to insure the goodness of Malt.

MALT'S HEALTHFUL VALUES are the welcome premium you enjoy in scores of Fun-Flavored foods and beverages. The maltose and dextrins of Barley Malt aid digestion . . . pick up lagging energies.

GOOD-FOR-YOU FACTORS include important B-complex vitamins and useful minerals. Good reason to look for Barley Malt in cereals, dairy drinks, baked goods, energy tonics and many other healthful products.

Write for free booklet, Homemaker's Guide to Barley Malt, Dept. 3, Barley & Malt Institute, 228 North LaSalle, Chicago 1, Illinois.

1959

The Statue Of Liberty Celebrates Her 75th Birthday.

WE HAVE OUR MEMORY PRIORITIES IN ORDER

Most Americans polled know who utters *"Hi Yo, Silver"* and *"What's Up Doc?"* but did not know who said *"I Have Not Yet Begun To Fight"* (John Paul Jones).

Martha Brunner Of Pittsburgh, Pennsylvania Is "Little Miss Muffin For 1959" In A Contest Sponsored By The Associated Retail Bakers Of America.

According to the New York Stock Exchange, 13 million Americans own stock.

HEAD OF THE CLASS(ES)

According to Dr. Harold M. Hodges, Jr., a sociologist at San Jose College, American society now consists of five social classes instead of three: **upper, upper-middle, lower-middle, upper-lower** and **lower-lower**.

U. S. POPULATION: 179 MILLION

Marriages: 1,494,000

Divorces: 396,000

HEY BUDDY, WE'VE GOT THIS GREAT DEAL ON SWAMP LAND

Land fever sweeps through Florida with lots of lots being sold via the mails.

Former President Harry S. Truman's Birthplace In Independence, Missouri, Is Dedicated As A National Shrine.

According to a recent study, most Americans want love and appreciation over wealth and fame.

U. S. And Soviets Will Exchange Artists In The Performing Arts For Exhibitions To Be Held In New York And Moscow.

The United States And The Soviets Agree On Cultural Exchange Including Arts, Science And Sports.

Pravda, The Soviet Newspaper, Treats Its Readers To The First Cartoon Of A Soviet Leader To Appear In The Russian Press.

HUSBAND HUNTING MADE DIFFICULT
A New Census Report Taken In The U.S.S.R. Reveals That There Are 55 Females For Every 45 Males.

'TILL MOSCOW FREEZES OVER

The First American Ice Show Goes To Russia.

A PIEROGI ON EVERY PLATE?
CIA Director Allen Dulles Challenges Khrushchev's Prediction That The U.S.S.R. Would Boast The World's Highest Standard Of Living In 11 Years.

DIVORCE EAST GERMAN STYLE
In East Germany a divorce can be granted on the grounds of "Anti-Marxism."

With More Than 10,000 East Berliners Streaming Into West Berlin Monthly, East Germany Becomes The Only Country In The World With A Steady Decrease In Its Population.

Volkswagen Factories Return To Private Ownership In West Germany.

A Salvage Team Discovers Nazi Gestapo Chief Heinrich Himmler's Personal Files And Diaries In Austria's Toplitz Lake.

DON'T LOCK HORNS WITH THIS COUNCILWOMAN

Protesting against the high cost of living, the electorate in Rio de Janeiro vote for their favorite write-in candidate for city council - Cacareco, the rhinoceros, who gets more votes than any other candidate. The winner is single and presently lives in the zoo.

NEXT THEY'LL BE WANTING SHOES

A constitutional amendment granting women voting privileges in national elections is defeated 2-1 by Swiss men.

3,500 WOMEN RECEIVE THE RIGHT TO VOTE in the old town of San Marino near Italy's Adriatic coast.

AMERICANS FAVOR CANADA
as their vacation destination over any other country in the world.

6,500 SYLVANIA FLASH BULBS erupt into one blinding burst as the 451-foot high Great Pyramid in the desert outside of Cairo is totally illuminated and photographed.

WHAT'S AN EIGHT LETTER WORD FOR BUSTED?

A ring of Americans and Canadians guilty of cheating on newspaper word puzzles by getting the answers in advance is broken up by the FBI.

Queen Elizabeth and President Eisenhower preside over the opening of the St. Lawrence Seaway, the world's greatest inland navigation system, linking the Great Lakes to the Atlantic. Canada's icebreaker "d'Iberville" unofficially opens the Seaway.

Tolls are established for the St. Lawrence Seaway.

The First Telephone Cable Linking North America And Europe Becomes Operational.

In An All-Out Effort To Get Brits To The Polls On Election Day, British Commercial Television Cancels All Western Programs That Day.

BEN JUST KEEPS TICKING AWAY London's **Big Ben Celebrates His 100th Anniversary.**

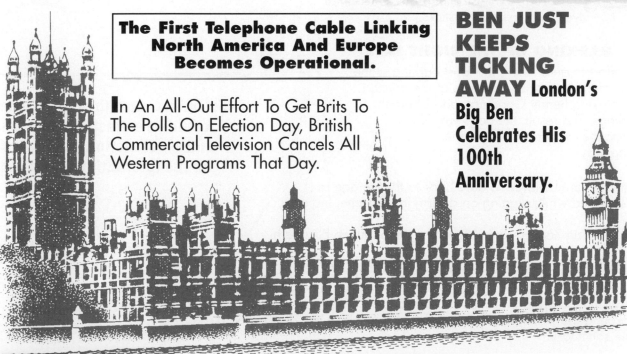

1959

NOT MUCH FIDDLIN' AROUND THESE DAYS

NERO'S GARDEN RUINS DISCOVERED IN ROME BY ARCHAEOLOGISTS.

SO WHAT'S BEEN HAPPENIN' MAN?

THE FIRST GREEK RULER SINCE 1439 CALLS ON THE POPE.

- **Heir to Jordan's kingdom, Amir Mohammed,** opens Aqaba, a Jordanian port.

- **Italian workers begin digging a tunnel** through Europe's highest mountain, Mont Blanc, which will decrease driving distance from Paris to Milan by several hundred miles.

- **Mexico and the United States** agree to build Diablo Dam on the Rio Grande.

- **Over 55 million women and children** in 105 countries receive help from UNICEF.

- **The International Red Cross turns 100.**

- **The Hague, Netherlands** is the home of the newly-formed International Society For Horticultural Science.

- **Spanish Jews** celebrate Rosh Hashana services in Madrid for the first time in 467 years.

- **World Refugee Year** commencing June 1959 is proclaimed by the U. N. General Assembly.

A 12-Nation Pact Is Signed In Washington Declaring Antarctica A Military-Free Preserve For Scientific Research.

 After two years of animal testing which produce evidence of injury, the Food And Drug Administration bans 17 coal-tar dyes used to color lipsticks.

BARKING UP THE RIGHT TREE

In an effort to quiet down the loud barking at the Toronto Humane Society, keepers of the pound begin playing Benny Goodman and Liberace recordings. The result: the dogs wag their tails, tap their paws and cease their barking ways.

- An elephant believed to date back to the ice-age is discovered while digging on a farm in Lafayette, Indiana.

- The London Zoo presents 12 flamingos to Queen Elizabeth.

PUT AWAY THOSE FISHING POLES, BOYS

In an action designed to protect its wildlife, the government of Ecuador declares the Galapagos Islands a national park with limited fishing rights in and around the waters surrounding the islands which are designated a marine sanctuary.

Scientists warn the Blue Whale could be extinct in five years unless restrictions are placed on the international whaling industry.

According to a recent report released by a Chicago bank, married women are better money managers than their husbands and make most of the buying decisions.

American Girls Marry At Youngest Age Of Industrialized Nations - 20.2 While The Men Marry By Age 23.

SOME SAY "I DO" AND THEY DO, WHILE SOME SAY "I DO" AND THEY DON'T

18% of American first marriages end in divorce—that's one in six— and one-third of second marriages also end up on the rocks.

RAISING THE ODDS

Chances For A Successful Marriage Are Higher When Men Marry Between Ages 25 To 30 And Women Between 23 To 28.

SHOULDN'T WE WAIT UNTIL OUR ZITS GO AWAY?

Teenage marriage (14-19-year olds) on the rise since World War II.

Polls indicate that most parents do not want their teenagers going steady too soon because of the emotional pressures it places on them.

RULES OF GOING STEADY

1. Exclusivity *(no dating others)*
2. Dancing only with each other *(unless they exchange dances with another couple)*
3. He can't leave her without a Saturday night date
4. He telephones her every night *(or have a reason why not)*
5. She must be at home to receive his call *(or have a reason why not)*

YOU ARE VERY DATABLE IF....

Weight and height in proportion.

Graceful bearing, stable and confident.

Neatly groomed hair and nails.

Sensible make-up.

Flattering clothing.

Tasteful accessories.

Pleasing voice.

Good sense of humor.

Good dancer.

Good listener.

TRAITS THAT WILL KEEP YOU HOME EVERY SATURDAY NIGHT:

Exaggerate or lie

Use foul language

Insist on having last word

Unreliable

Pout when you can't have your own way

Drink too much

Make disparaging remarks about older people

Exhibitionist behavior

Make negative comments about men

61% of college girls polled expected to work after marriage with 11% of them planning a career and marriage.

According to the Royal Society of Health at Harrogate, England the happiest mothers are women with careers.

Sociologists out of the Boston and Michigan areas conclude that working wives tend to be bossier than their stay-at-home counterparts.

Married women with children tend to derive more satisfaction from housework than their unmarried counterparts who view it more as plain old drudgery.

WAYS A SINGLE CAREER WOMAN CAN FIND HAPPINESS

- Buy A Home
- Get A Roommate
- Have Hobbies
- Participate In Community Activities
- Develop Social Skills (Bridge, Golf, Dancing)
- Make More Friends
- Strengthen Family Ties

HEY BABY, WANNA GET ME ANOTHER BEER

According to a psychologist at University of California, men who are glib talkers with polished speech and social grace are not as masculine as those men who are not as articulate.

WHY CAN'T A MAN BE MORE LIKE A WOMAN?

According to a recent study, in an effort to be a "today" kind of guy, American men are tapping more and more into their feminine side, developing such traits as warmth, dependence, compliance.

AT LAST, SOMETHING BOTH SEXES CAN AGREE ON

Recent Surveys Reveal That Both Men And Women Agree That Women Are More Extravagant Than Men.

A British research team names the following women as beautiful but can't come up with a formula that clearly defines beauty:

PHYSICAL BEAUTY: Ingrid Bergman, Grace Kelly, Marilyn Monroe, Elizabeth Taylor

SPIRITUAL BEAUTY: Helen Keller

THE WORLD'S MOST BEAUTIFUL WOMEN
(BY COUNTRY)

Italy
France
Sweden
Spain
United States

100% FRESH
NEW DELCO DC-7

$15⁹⁵

6 VOLT EXCHANGE

Ask for the DC-7! It's the new low cost addition to Delco's fine line of dry charge batteries. Like all Delco Dry Charge batteries, the DC-7 can't get old before it's sold. It's kept factory-fresh, dry as a bone. When you buy it, you see the dealer add the activator fluid, so you know you're getting all the power you pay for! Ask your dealer for the new Delco DC-7 . . . *extra starts at no extra cost.*

6- AND 12-VOLT MODELS FOR ALL CARS — A GENERAL MOTORS WARRANTY GOOD ALL OVER THE UNITED STATES AND CANADA

QUALITY BUILT BY DELCO-REMY, AVAILABLE EVERYWHERE THROUGH *GENERAL MOTORS STARTS WITH DELCO BATTERIES*

President Eisenhower breaks ground for new $75 million Lincoln Center For The Performing Arts in New York which will house a new Metroplitan Opera House, New York Philharmonic and the Juilliard School Of Music.

U. S. citizenship is restored to almost 5,000 Japanese who renounced it during World War II.

The last surviving veteran of the **Civil War** is **Walter Williams**, and his death at 117 is mourned throughout the nation.

Harvard and Yale withdraw from the National Defense Education Program in protest over students applying for student loans being required to sign affidavits denying they are subversives.

Congress passes first law authorizing the leasing of Indian tribal lands.

STILL NO SIPPING IN MISSIS-SIP-PI

Mississippi Is The Only Remaining Dry State After Oklahoma Voters Dump Prohibition.

Your Home Can Now Be Invaded Without A Warrant By U. S. Health Inspectors According To The Supreme Court.

OFF WITH THOSE HOODS

California's Governor Pat Brown Signs Law Making It Illegal To Wear Glasses That Restrict Lateral Vision While Driving.

Use Of Radar To Check Speed And Authority To Conduct Blood Tests To Determine If Someone Is Legally Intoxicated Being Sought By Governor Pat Brown.

Judge Learned Hand Celebrates His 50th Year Sitting On The Federal Bench.

President Eisenhower Extends Peacetime Draft Until July 1, 1963.

President Eisenhower Initiates Study That Assigns Responsibility For The Protection Of Americans From Atomic Radiation.

Despite the fact that 341 women now sit in state legislatures across the country, in a poll of newspaper women's page editors, most of whom are female, 25% are opposed to a woman holding the office of United States vice-president while the balance named **Margaret Chase Smith**, **Clare Boothe Luce** and **Eleanor Roosevelt** as favorite candidates for the vice-presidency.

HEY, WHAT ABOUT DAISIES - LIKE IN PUSHING UP
A battle is raging on the floor of the U. S. Senate over the choice for national flower with vehement support for the Corn Tassel, Rose, Carnation or Grass.

WHAT A YEAR IT WAS!

WE ARE THE MEN FROM TEXACO

Texaco Inc. is now the new name of the Texas Co.

20,000 Pounds Of Cranberries

From Oregon And Washington Potentially Tainted With Weed Killer Are Given Clean Bill Of Health Just In Time For Thanksgiving Tables.

BEATNIK & NUDNIK CORNER

Much to the chagrin of the neighborhood, a Beatnik by the name of **Eric ("Big Daddy")** turns an abandoned bingo parlor near Venice Beach, California into a coffee house called **"The Gas House"**—a haven for music and poetry.

"Sick" comedians, **Mort Sahl, Jonathan Winters, Shelley Berman, Tom Lehrer, Don Adams** and newcomer **Lenny Bruce** pack in nightclub audiences across the country.

ODE TO MY RAPIDLY DETERIORATING FAVORITE PET MANGO

Those bourgeois bucks roll in for San Francisco's City Lights Book Store/publishing company run by Beatnik poet **Lawrence Ferlinghetti**, ("A Coney Island Of The Mind") as the "straight" world eats up words by Beat poets **Allen Ginsberg**, ("Howl") **Jack Kerouac**, ("The Subterraneans") **Gregory Corso**, ("Gasoline") **Bob Kaufman** ("Second April") and **Vachel Lindsay** ("The Congo").

AND THE REVEREND SAID: "LET US CREATE A PLACE FOR THE CREATIVE AND THEY WILL COME"

It's Saturday night at Rev. Pierre Delattre's "The Bread And Wine Mission" in the North Beach section of San Francisco and poets show up by the hundreds to read their poetry to a background of softly glowing candles, cigarettes, wine and acceptance.

A SHONDER, A SHONDER ME THINKS THE LADY NOT A BEATNIK BE—

Bathing suit clad beautiful Broadway chorus girl **Gerry Crotty** wins Miss Beatnik 1959 contest much to the dismay of the other contestants who are more appropriately attired for the competition wearing old dungarees and sneakers.

WHAT A YEAR IT WAS!

furs by Revillon

Wherever automobiles are seen and appreciated, the Cadillac name has, over the years, become an accepted synonym for "quality". Yet never before has the Cadillac car represented such a *high* standard of excellence as it does today. In its great beauty and majesty . . . in its fineness of performance . . . in the elegance of its Fleetwood interiors . . . and in the skill of its craftsmanship . . . it is far and away the finest fruit of Cadillac's unending quest for quality. We believe that a personal inspection will convince you of this fact—and that an hour at the wheel will add certainty to conviction. Why not accept your dealer's invitation to visit him soon—for a ride and a revelation?

CADILLAC MOTOR CAR DIVISION • GENERAL MOTORS CORPORATION
EVERY WINDOW OF EVERY CADILLAC IS SAFETY PLATE GLASS

Cadillac ...world's best synonym for quality!

BUSINESS

FORD
DROPS ITS
SUPER LEMON
THE
EDSEL

As the **National Debt** approaches the legal limit fixed by Congress of $295 billion, approximately each of the 176,665,000 Americans will owe roughly $1,641.52 to the future.

Labor Department Announces Record Employment Of 68 Million With Less Than One Worker In 20 Out Of Work Compared To Last Year's 1 Out Of 15.

McCall's Magazine
Becomes First National Women's Magazine To Include A Special Western Edition.

Hormel + Co.
Produces Its
Billionth Can Of
SPAM

☞ **U. S. ATLANTIC AND GULF COAST PORTS** almost entirely shut down due to International Longshoremen strike.

☞ **IN THE LONGEST NATIONWIDE STEEL STRIKE** in America's history, and the 6th since World War II, 500,000 steelworkers strike as union and management fail to reach an agreement closing down 85% of the nation's steel output.

☞ **GENERAL MOTORS** ceases automobile production due to strike.

☞ **1,100 HOSPITAL EMPLOYEES** representing seven major New York hospitals go out on an unparalleled 45-day strike.

☞ **STRIKING AMERICAN AIRLINES PILOTS** settle a three-week strike which idles 18,000 other employees resulting in $34 million in lost earnings and salaries.

☞ **NEW YORKERS HAVE TO MUDDLE THROUGH** for 19 days without their favorite newspaper as a deliverymen's strike closes down the city's nine major dailies with a total circulation of 5.7 million.

☞ **6,000 CHICAGO TEACHERS** go on strike for, and win, a $500 annual increase, making them the highest paid city teachers in the country.

1959

Senator
Robert A. Taft,
author of
Taft-Hartly act.

Taft-Hartly Injunction to end steel strike ordered by U. S. District Court in Pittsburgh and stayed by U. S. 3rd Circuit Court Of Appeals.

President Eisenhower names a board to inquire into the steel dispute after invoking the Taft-Hartly Act.

Taft-Hartly Injunction against steel strike upheld by U. S. Supreme Court.

Readmission Of International Longshoremen on a two-year probation is authorized by the A.F.L.-C.I.O.

American Federation Of Television And Radio Artists and the Screen Actors Guild vote to merge into one union with a combined membership of 25,000.

Congress Passes First Major Labor Law since the 1947 Taft-Hartly act as a result of the McClellan Committee hearings which investigated union corruption. With Robert F. Kennedy acting as chief counsel, Teamsters' head Jimmy Hoffa is called to testify many times but is evasive and falls under a barrage of criticism for not cleaning up his union.

President Of United Mine Workers since 1919, **John L. Lewis** announces his plan to resign in 1960.

John L. Lewis

WHAT A YEAR IT WAS!

Studebaker-Packard joins the small car market with the debut of its Lark model.

- Ford beats Chrysler by a beak as they both register the name "Falcon."

- The success of the Rambler pulls American Motors out of the red for the first time in six years.

- Grand Jury investigation of General Motors under the antitrust laws is ordered by U. S. Justice Department.

American Airlines announces that its Boeing 707 airliners have been flying nearly 100% full.

The Long Island Railroad celebrates its 125th birthday and spruces up its insignia.

First class and deluxe passengers will now be able to order from 36 different meals being offered on Swissair.

Chemical Corn Exchange And **New York Trust** Merge To Form **Chemical Bank New York Trust Co.** Making It New York's Third Largest Bank.

Two Banking Institutions Merge, **J. P. Morgan Co.** And **Guaranty Trust Co.,** Forming **Morgan Guaranty Trust**, Creating The Fourth Largest Bank In The Country.

BUY NOW AND PAY LATER

The **Bank of America** Introduces The First American Revolving Credit Card Allowing Minimum Monthly Payments With The Balance Carried Over To The Following Month With Interest Added.

Passings

NEWSWEEK creator and heir to one of the great fortunes of all time, businessman and philanthropist **Vincent Astor** dies at age 67.

Chairman of Pepsi-Cola and Joan Crawford's husband, **Alfred N. Steele**, dies of a heart attack in New York at age 57.

The first woman president of Lord & Taylor, **Dorothy Shaver**, dies of a stroke at age 61.

New Jersey Mail-Order House, Free Film Co., Acts As Broker For Several Photo Finishers Providing Free Film With Developed Pictures To The Consumer Who Skips Their Neighborhood Drugstore, Allowing Them To Save At Least 40% In Developing Charges.

A record $68 billion is spent on life insurance.

Los Angeles plans to revitalize its downtown area with the $339 million Bunker Hill project.

A group of American textile machinery companies signs a contract with the Soviet Union to provide and install equipment for spinning and weaving factories.

McDonnell Aircraft in St. Louis is awarded a $15 million space exploration contract.

Ground is broken in Lake Maracaibo, Venezuela for new $3 million flour mill in a joint venture between Pillsbury Co. and Latin American industrialist Eugenio Mendoza Goiticoa.

78% of the nation's 370,000 college seniors have already found jobs with electrical engineers being the most desired for technical positions.

THE DOW-JONES industrial average passes the 600 mark and continues to rise to 678.10.

THE FUNCTION OF CLEARING TRANSACTIONS for the American Stock Exchange is assigned to a new machine.

FAMILY-OWNED NEIMAN-MARCUS stock is offered to the public for the first time at $19.50.

Hollywood Actress **Joan Crawford Steel** *Is Elected To Pepsi-Cola's Board Of Directors To Fill Opening Left By The Death Of Her Husband Alfred, Chairman Of The Board.*

Mrs. Josephine Bay, Financier And Sportswoman Of New York And Palm Beach, Is Elected Chairman Of American Export Lines, Inc. Becoming First Woman To Head Major Ship Line.

PLAYING KETCH-UP
The First Non-Family Member To Become President Of H. J. Heinz Co. Is **Frank R. Armour, Jr.,** *50, Who Started Out As A Visitors' Guide In 1927.*

Growing Demand For
Coconut Oil
Causes Sharp Increase In Price.

this was the price that was

UNDER $1.00

Aspirin, 100 ct.	$ .49
Ball Pen.	1.00
Carnegie Hall (lowest priced ticket)	.60
Cough Syrup	.49
Eyelash Curler	1.00
Life Savers	.05

Life Magazine	$ .25
Lipstick	.79
Magic Marker	.77
Movie Ticket (child)	.50
Nail Polish	.49
Public Drunkenness Fine (London)	.70
Toothpaste	.88
Tweezers	.29

HOME NECESSITIES

Baby Stroller	$ 24.95
Clothes Hamper	5.95
Fountain Pen	2.95
Mattress, Posturepedic	79.50
Movie Projector	89.95
Play Pen (portable)	24.95
Sewing Machine (portable)	69.50
Stereo	39.95
Radio (transistor pocket)	34.95
Television w/remote control	199.95
Vacuum Cleaner	49.50

THE ULTIMATE KITCHEN

Blender	$ 34.95
Double Boiler	11.75
Electric Range	149.00

Iron	$ 16.95
Percolator	17.95
Skillet	16.95
Tea Kettle	4.95
Toaster	29.95

FOR HIM

Boxer Shorts	$ 1.65
Haircut: Los Angeles	2.00
New York	1.50
Shoes	7.95-19.95
Slacks	10.98
Socks	1.00
Sports Shirt	2.99
Suit, worsted	65.00
Tie, silk	2.95
Topcoat	65.00

New York Rentals

5 room apartment in Flushing: $150.00

4 room apartment in Jamaica: $115.00

3½ room apartment in Rego Park: $135.00

2 family house in Bensonhurst: $125.00

FOR HER

Bermuda Shorts	$ 10.95
Capri Pants	5.98
Cardigan	5.98
Dress (Italian wool knit)	35.00
Dress (pleated jersey)	14.98
Espadrilles	2.50
Girdle	12.50
Gloves	4.98
Handbag (straw)	$ 16.95
Hat (velvet & rayon)	16.95
Housecoat (silk brocade)	25.00
Pedal Pushers	4.98
Petticoat	5.99
Shoes (imported)	30.95-45.00
Toreador Pajamas	6.95

AUTOMOBILES

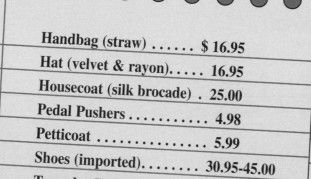

Edsel Station Wagon	$ 2,971.00
VW Bug	1,675.00
Mercedes Benz, 300 SL Roadster	10,978.00
Volvo	2,390.00
Jaguar Mark IX	6,200.00

FOOD

American Cheese (lb.)	$ .51
Apples (lb.)	.16
Butter (lb.)	.77
Coffee (lb.)	.78
Corn (10 ears)	.25
Honeydew Melon (ea.)	.59
Iceberg Lettuce	.19
Milk (qt.)	.27
Oreo Cookies (11 oz.)	.33
Peanut Butter (12 oz.)	.35
Sugar (lb.)	.11
Vegetable Oil (qt.)	.45
Watermelon (lb.)	.04

Count Sarmi lines a silk crepe de chine kimono with flowery brocade to interpret the double luxury of "negligee pink" Soft-Weve, the bathroom tissue with the exquisite "facial quality" and delicate colors.

To match the luxurious 2-ply softness of snowy white Soft-Weve, Sybil Connolly of Dublin lavishes yards of crush-pleated Irish linen and hand-crocheted lace on this heavenly soft negligee.

Scaasi designs a younger-than-springtime "angel-wing" confection in Soft-Weve "negligee pink." *See* the softness, *see* how lovely Soft-Weve pastels are — right through their new transparent wrap!

The most noticed little luxury in your home

Soft-Weve®

2-PLY TISSUE BY SCOTT

SCOTT
soft-weve
FACIAL QUALITY
TWO-PLY TISSUE

NEW! "See-through" wrap

Fold on fold of silken-soft taffeta in a negligee designed by Count Sarmi to match "negligee green" Soft-Weve. See *all* the delicate colors with new Soft-Weve perforations, so neat and easy-to-tear.

Shimmery Grecian negligee—a slim, silvery vision in softest lamé chiffon. Specially designed by Yanni to match the heavenly softness of "facial quality" Soft-Weve in delicate "negligee blue."

With softest silk faille and satin, Ferreras creates a luxurious court-train peignoir strewn with French roses—specially designed to match the softness and delicacy of "negligee yellow" Soft-Weve.

"Pour on the goodness with Borden's Half and Half!"

says Elsie, the Borden Cow

Borden's Half and Half is richer than milk (and more satisfying), lighter than cream (lower in calories).

Use it to put real country-goodness into scrambled eggs, smooth gravies, soups and puddings.

Get Borden's Half and Half in the pint size at your neighborhood store or from your Borden man. You can buy Borden's Half and Half in Ontario and Quebec, too.

And remember, Borden's has a cream for every purpose: Light Cream, Heavy Cream and Sour Cream.

If it's

Borden's

it's *got* to be good!

See Borden's TV shows "Ruff and Reddy" and "Fury" over NBC.   © The Borden Co.

WHAT A YEAR IT WAS!

ENTERTAINMENT

Boat Tour Around Manhattan Island	$ 2.50
Hotel & Food, Catskills, New York	189.00/wk.
Hotel Room, Essex House, Manhattan	13.00 and up
Opera Ticket, Covent Garden, London	11.76

SALARIES
yearly

Average Family	$ 6,600.00
Average Pay, New College Grads	5,268.00
Congressman	22,500.00
Copywriter	5,200.00
Doctor (city)	25,000.00
Doctor (country)	12,000.00
Top Fashion Models	25,000.00-60,000.00

weekly

Dance Teacher	$ 102.00
Dictaphone Operator	85.00
Elevator Operator	55.00
Gal Friday	75.00
Hollywood Screenwriter	9,000.00

other

Marilyn Monroe, "Some Like It Hot"	$ 300,000.00

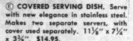
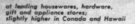

SCIENCE & MEDICINE

DID YOU HEAR THE ONE ABOUT NURSE GLUTZ?

Dr. Rose L. Coser, sociologist at McLean Hospital, Belmont, Mass., observes that laughter acts as an outlet for anger and dissatisfaction for hospitalized patients allowing them to entertain and comfort each other.

Harvard Sociologist Professor Alex Inkeles Claims That Frequent Laughter Is A Sign Of High Social Status.

A Social Scientist From The University Of Michigan predicts that **SCIENTIFIC ADVANCES** will **PEAK IN 1973** and then **SLOW DOWN** around the year **2055**.

A LOOK AT THE WORLD AT THE TURN OF THE CENTURY
— Y E A R   2 0 0 0 —

Scientists at the Stanford Reseach Institute report on the rapid development of peacetime science and suggest the following are among the many sobering results of present research:

1. Rocket Mail Service
2. Synthetic Coffee & Tea
3. Climate Control
4. Radio Broadcasts Relayed By Space Satellite
5. Teaching Machines
6. Brain Control
7. Mine The Ocean Floor
8. Further Development Of Oral Contraceptives
9. Chemical Food Pills

WHAT A YEAR IT WAS!

With Eight Million People With A Drinking Problem, One-Fifth Of Whom Are Women, Alcoholism Is The Nation's Third Largest Health Problem With 500,000 New Alcoholics Emerging Annually.

WHAT THEY NEED IS W.A. (WATER ANONYMOUS)

Britain reports on the "Hydrolic," a compulsive water drinker who consumes 30 - 35 pints of the clear stuff a day and exhibits many of the same outward symptoms of a drunk including the next-day hangover.

CITING EINSTEIN AND FREUD AS EXAMPLES, according to University of Wisconsin geneticist Dr. William Harold Stone, Jews possess superior intelligence precisely because they "have been isolated by geographical, cultural and religious barriers" thus keeping their gene pool from co-mingling with other gene pools which may have less of a propensity for pursuing intellectual or analytical careers.

MY SON, THE PROFESSOR

UNIVERSITY OF CALIFORNIA PROFESSOR, HANS ALBERT EINSTEIN, son of Albert, is honored by the American Society of Civil Engineers for outstanding research on transportation of sediment in flowing water.

❏ French geneticist Jerome Lejeune traces an extra chromosome as the cause of mental and physical handicaps of people afflicted with Down's Syndrome.

❏ HIV tainted blood is given by a Bantu man from Central Africa at a hospital clinic in the Belgian Congo.

❏ Frozen bone marrow cells are now available for the first time through a technique developed by the Veterans Administration.

❏ 300 plant and animal viruses have been identified — 80 in the past ten years.

Successful Testing Is Reported By Nobel Prize Winner, **Dr. John F. Enders,** On Children Who Develop Antibodies After Being Given A Live-Virus Measles Vaccine.

A New Survey Concludes That Salt Is A Major Contributor To High Blood Pressure.

In a dig in Western Libya, Dr. Fabrizio Mori of the Italian Institute of Prehistory And Protohistory discovers preserved body of a child thought to be over 5,400-years old, making it the oldest mummy ever discovered.

Man-ape skull fragments thought to be 600,000 to 1 million years old are discovered in Tanganyika's Olduvai Gorge by British anthropologist Louis S. B. Leakey.

Columbia University announces the discovery of a submarine plateau more than double the size of Connecticut in the Arctic Ocean.

Combining Features From Around 50,000 Photographs,
Los Angeles Detective H. C. McDonald's **"Identikit"** Leads To Its First Arrest.

RUN FOR THOSE EAR-PLUGS
The General Electric research laboratory creates the highest pitch sound ever reported.

BUSINESS-SPEAK
Businesses see the introduction of COBOL, a computer software language designed for business use.

RCA is developing new electronic computing techniques approaching the operating limits imposed by the speed of light.

Singer Military Products introduces a motion detector device that can identify and measure movement thousands of feet away.

THE WORLD'S LARGEST INSECT
—a 4-inch long beetle with an 8-inch wing span—is on display at New York's American Museum of Natural History where spectators watch as he peels a banana with his horns and then munches away on Chiquita's finest.

1959

ON THE THRESHOLD OF SPACE

Competing with 110 candidates, the first test pilots chosen to be astronauts for Project Mercury's man-in-space program are introduced at a NASA press conference:

(left to right) **Scott Carpenter, Gordon Cooper, John Glenn, Gus Grissom, Wally Schirra, Alan Shepard** and **Deke Slayton.**

Astronauts Will Feast On A Liquid Meal Comprised Of Ham, Chicken And Steak Created For Space Travel By The U. S. Army.

NASA presents its long-range space program to U. S. Congress.

•

President Eisenhower presents 10-year space program to U. S. Congress for the launching of U. S. satellites or space-probe vehicles.

•

Backed by Secretary of the Department of Health, Education and Welfare, Arthur S. Flemming, **women scientists** warn that the space race will be lost if America doesn't take advantage of female brain-power and urge science and engineering deans to accept more women.

Moscow announces that its moon rocket has soared past the moon and will orbit around the sun as man's first artificial planet.

September: History is made as Russia's Luna 2 hits the moon 35 hours after the launch.

October: Luna 3 photographs far side of the moon for first time revealing less craters than face.

After studying moon shots taken last year by Soviet astronomer N. A. Kozyrev, American astrophysicists confirm lunar volcanic activity.

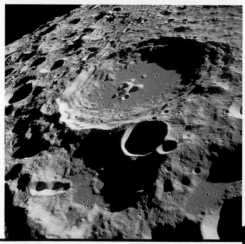

NASA launches **Explorer VII** at Cape Canaveral.

Explorer VI, U. S. paddle-wheel satellite, takes first T.V. pictures of earth's cloud covering.

U. S. lunar probe **Pioneer IV** is launched and heads into orbit around the sun.

Discoverer I written off by scientists as missing.

NASA to use satellites for transcontinental radio.

Vanguard III is launched out of Cape Canaveral as a weather satellite becoming the 12th successfully launched U. S. satellite.

The U. S. launches a satellite eye to scan the atmosphere as an aid in predicting weather conditions.

Hughes Aircraft Co. is developing an atomic clock for use in a space satellite that will not gain or lose a second in 1,000 years.

Juno II rocket, the launch vehicle for Pioneer and Explorer satellites.

Below, Explorer facilities being inspected by key personnel.

- British Jet Plane Flies Twice As Fast As The Speed Of Sound.
- The Largest Radio Telescope In The World Goes Under Construction In The West Virginia Mountains Which Will Boast A Range Of 38 Billion Light Years.
- For The First Time, Nike Anti-Aircraft Missile Successfully Fired From Canadian Soil.
- Atlas Ballistic Missile Announced Operational With First Training Flight Being Conducted From Vandenberg Air Force Base.
- Thor And Jupiter Intermediate-Range Ballistic Missiles Become Operational.
- First Radar Contact Is Made With Venus By The MIT Lincoln Lab.
- 800 Teenagers Attend A Rocket Seminar At New York University's Bronx Campus Sponsored By Military And Non-Military Experts.

PRESS THE BUTTON ABLE...NO! NOT THAT BUTTON, THE OTHER ONE!

Two female monkeys, Able and Baker, are successfully launched into space returning alive and well. Space monkey Able later dies during operation to have her cerebral electrode removed.

The Soviets announce two dogs and a rabbit are returned safely after space travel.

WHAT A YEAR IT WAS!

1959

 Radioactivity increases up to 300% in Eastern United States following the Soviet's nuclear tests in September 1958.

 The Soviets and the United States sign agreement on joint nuclear research program.

 Russia announces extension of nuclear test ban as long as the U. S. and Great Britain do not resume testing.

 Six American atomic authorities spend almost two weeks investigating Russian nuclear equipment.

THE SOVIET ICEBREAKER, "LENIN," THE WORLD'S FIRST NUCLEAR-POWERED SURFACE SHIP, IS LAUNCHED IN LENINGRAD.

THE WORLD'S FIRST NUCLEAR-POWERED MERCHANT SHIP, THE "SAVANNAH," IS LAUNCHED IN CAMDEN, NEW JERSEY.

FIRST U.S. NUCLEAR SUB WITH BALLISTIC MISSILES — "GEORGE WASHINGTON" — IS LAUNCHED.

U.S. NUCLEAR SUB "SKATE" COMPLETES ITS SECOND RUN UNDER THE NORTH POLE.

THE "SEAWOLF" STAYS SUBMERGED FOR TWO MONTHS WHILE THE NUCLEAR-POWERED "SKIPJACK" SETS DEPTH RECORD OF BELOW 400 FEET AND SPEED RECORD FOR THAT DEPTH OF OVER 20 KNOTS.

THE FIRST NUCLEAR REACTOR FOR MEDICAL TREATMENT and research is built at Brookhaven National Laboratory, Upton, Long Island, New York.

PENNSYLVANIA STATE UNIVERSITY PHYSICIST invents the ion microscope making it possible to explore the atom.

STANFORD UNIVERSITY TO BE HOME of a two-mile long linear accelerator to be used as a research facility according to an announcement made by the Atomic Energy Commission.

UNIVERSITY OF CALIFORNIA AT BERKELEY is the home of new radiation laboratory where some of the world's most complicated and dangerous scientific instruments are ready to become operational.

GENERAL ELECTRIC builds a 15-foot atom smasher in Schenectady, New York.

GENERAL DYNAMICS CORPORATION builds John Jay Hopkins Research Laboratory near San Diego for its atomic division.

ATOMIC ENERGY COMMISSION UNVEILS atomic generator tinier than a man's hat.

CONSOLIDATED EDISON'S $100,000,000 atomic energy plant at Indian Point, New York is 50% completed.

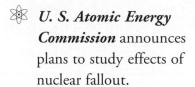

* **U. S. Atomic Energy Commission** announces plans to study effects of nuclear fallout.

* **Water samples taken from the Animas River** in Colorado and New Mexico found to contain levels of radium as high as 160% over safety levels as a result of run-off from the Vanadium Corp. of America refinery plant.

* **"Look Back In Anger" author John Osborne** participates in campaign for nuclear disarmament in Britain.

* **Princeton University's Dr. E. P. Wigner** receives the Atomic Energy Commission's Enrico Fermi Award for work in development of nuclear reactors related to atom research.

* **The $75,000 "Atoms For Peace" award** goes to 73-year old Hungarian Professor George de Hevesy.

* **With the aid of the Soviet Union,** Hungary's first atomic reactor is completed.

WHAT A YEAR IT WAS!

NOBEL PRIZE WINNER LINUS PAULING ESTIMATES THAT AMERICA HAS A CACHE OF 75,000 NUCLEAR WEAPONS.

Automatically Controlled Automobiles Demonstrated In A Model Created By The General Motors Research Laboratories.

Illinois Bell Telephone Develops A Three-Ounce Heart Device Which Measures The Patient's Heartbeats For A Full Day.

A Six Ounce Heart Monitor Is Developed By Dr. William F. Veling Of Detroit.

NEITHER A SHIP NOR AN AIRPLANE BE
Britain's Saunders-Roe, Ltd. Unveils Its Hovercraft, A Vehicle That Travels Above Land Or Water Surface On A Cushion Of Air.

France's Undersea Photographer, Jacques Cousteau, Develops Water Craft Capable Of Descending 1,600 Feet With Two Aboard.

Timed Stop Lights Indicating the Amount Of Time A Motorist Has To Cross The Street Is Introduced In Tokyo.

Rx

- Tests Begin To Determine Whether Or Not Live Polio Virus Vaccine Is Better Than The Salk Vaccine.

- The Mayo Clinic Reports That Large Doses Of Niacin Is Most Effective Way Of Reducing Blood Cholesterol Levels.

- An AMA Study Indicates That Pep Pills Or Amphetamines Stimulate Athletes To Higher Performance Levels But Have Serious Side Effects Including Dependency And Weight Loss.

INVENTOR OF THE POLIO VACCINE, DR. JONAS SALK RECEIVES HONORARY DOCTOR OF SCIENCE DEGREE AT LEEDS UNIVERSITY.

- A New Neomycin-Hydrocortisone Ointment Found Very Effective In Reducing Swelling, Tenderness And Stiffness Caused By Injuries.

- A Combination Of Rinsing With Hydrogen-Peroxide And Antihistimine Pills Clears Up Trench Mouth In Three Days.

SURGICAL ADVANCES

Tracheal fenestration, a new procedure in which a windpipe opening is made in the neck for access for suctioning mucus and delivering medication, is developed at New York Medical College by Dr. E. E. Rockey.

A Texas child's toe is transplanted to the thumb area by Dr. B.S. Freeman of Houston following an accident that severed the thumb from the rest of the hand.

Toronto's Dr. Samuel W. Leslie performs the first successful tooth transplant transferring a tooth from a young girl to her older brother.

The Rand Development Corp. of Cleveland negotiates with Russia to manufacture their suturing gun and surgical color camera for American distribution.

the CANCER front

* Dr. Ernest L. Wynder Of The Sloan-Kettering Institute Of Cancer Research In New York Identifies Two New Factors In Cigarette Tar Produce Cancer In Laboratory Animals Raising The Number Of Cancer-Causing Compounds To Eight.

* America Is Spending Upwards Of $100,000,000 On Cancer Research Being Carried Out By 6,000 Scientists.

* The National Cancer Institute Estimates That Cancer Will Strike 450,000 Americans By Year-End With 260,000 Deaths.

* Lung Cancer, With A Lower Cure Rate, Is The Fastest Rising Kind Of Cancer And Will Kill 35,000 Americans This Year - 85% Of Them Men.

HOW ABOUT SEWING THE LIPS TOGETHER?

In Their Quest To Drop Those Extra Few Pounds, Americans Spend Upwards Of $100,000,000 A Year On Ineffective Diet Aids.

MEN BATTLE THE BULGE

While Today's 25-Year Old Woman Weighs Five Pounds Less Than Her Mom At The Same Age, Her Male Counterpart Weighs At Least Five Pounds More Than His Dad Did At 25.

Dr. Jean Mayer Of The Harvard School Of Public Health States That Many Plump People Inherit Their Inclination To Be Fat.

Milk Is The Favorite Food Of Soldiers Stationed At Fort Carson, Colorado.

According To A Recently Released Two-Year Study Conducted In Great Britain, Children Who Eat An Apple A Day Experienced Half The Amount Of Tooth Decay Than Their Non-Apple Eating Counterparts.

Americans Have Altered Their Eating Patterns Over The Last 50 Years Eating A Greater Selection Of Foods Containing Essential Nutrients Such As Milk, Meat, Poultry And Eggs.

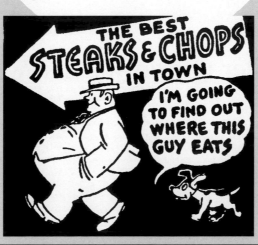

THE BEST STEAKS & CHOPS IN TOWN

I'M GOING TO FIND OUT WHERE THIS GUY EATS

Fems
FEMININE NAPKINS

Now! A longer napkin you can wear and forget!

Shop, work, play as you please.

At long last here's a feminine napkin you can wear and forget!

Fems feminine napkins are longer to fit better and absorb better. Yet, there's not an ounce of extra bulk.

Now your protection stays put even under stress, thanks to the extra length of the tab ends. What a feeling of security!

Forget about stains. Wear your best party dress, knowing there's a protective safety-cushion to prevent accidents, whether you're seated or moving about.

Forget about shifting and binding. Longer Fems feminine napkins are made to adjust to your body without discomfort—no matter how active you may be.

Forget about chafing. Touch the chafe-free covering to the inside of your wrist, where your skin is extra sensitive. No wonder Fems bring welcome relief from chafing.

Fems absorb quickly. That's another protection against chafing. And both the covering and inner materials are designed to keep surfaces comfortably dry, even during the heaviest flow.

Would you pay a few cents more for all this comfort and confidence? Of course you would!

Next time wear Fems—and forget!

FEMS is a trademark of Kimberly-Clark Corp.

PSYCHIATRY

Scientific Evidence Seems To Indicate That Mental Powers Don't Decline After Middle Age.

ACTING CAN BE DANGEROUS TO YOUR MENTAL HEALTH

According to a famous Hollywood psychiatrist more than half of Hollywood's actors and actresses will experience mental health problems.

SMILE THOUGH YOUR HEART IS BREAKING

In a study of American entertainers conducted by two sociologists at the University of Texas, it is revealed that while more than one-third of America's most successful entertainers experienced difficult childhoods, comedians had the most difficult time as kids, with more than 40% of them coming from broken homes and 70% of them experiencing poverty as youngsters.

Philadelphia psychologist Dr. Carlton W. Orchinik notes that children who stutter are more likely to have been tickled hard by a parent of the opposite sex.

According to a report issued by the National Institute of Mental Health, one out of sixteen Americans will suffer a mental illness.

Because Of Long Hours Of Isolation, The Personality Type Best Suited For A Spaceman Is An Introvert.

VE VANT TO BE ALONE

A staff psychiatrist for San Francisco's Veterans Hospital defines "Beatniks" as not necessarily sick of life but like any group of sick people just want to be left alone.

The Mental Research Institute of Palo Alto, California begins operation.

According to Dr. Lewis J. Sherman, Veterans Hospital, Brockton, Massachusetts, psychopathic criminals tend to have better memories than normal or neurotic people because the psychopath isn't beset by memory-blocking anxieties.

With The Pursuit Of Materialism Coupled With Expanding Technology, Americans And Europeans Are Destined To Suffer From A "Mass Neurosis" Unless The Pace Of Modern Life Slows Down According To A British And A Canadian Scientist.

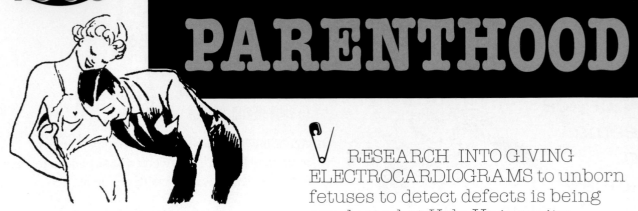

PARENTHOOD

BETTER NOT BE MORE THAN KISSIN' CUZINS

Researchers Conclude That When First Cousins Marry, The Death Rate For Their Children Is About Three Times Higher Than Unrelated Parents And The Incidence Of Abnormalities Is About Double The Average.

The National Safety Council Reports That 30 Small Children Died In Several Months From Suffocation Caused By Playing With Plastic Bags Precipitating A Nationwide Campaign To Alert Parents To The Dangers Of Allowing Their Children To Play With Plastic Bags Used In Dry Cleaning.

The Traditional RABBIT TEST May Be Replaced With A Newly-Developed Hormone-Pill Test For Pregnancy Promising Much Greater Accuracy.

RESEARCH INTO GIVING ELECTROCARDIOGRAMS to unborn fetuses to detect defects is being conducted at Yale University.

ACCORDING TO AN ARTICLE appearing in "Postgraduate Medicine," despite all the modern conveniences at home, the demands of motherhood are greater than ever causing many moms to experience fatigue dubbed "tired mother syndrome."

STUDIES AT THE PHILADELPHIA LYING-IN HOSPITAL reveal that taller women give birth to bigger babies.

TRANQUILIZER PHENERGAN used during childbirth to lessen pain.

ONE OUT OF EVERY 5,000 BRITONS are test tube babies.

ACCORDING TO A PEDIATRICIAN at Northwestern University, colicky infants generally emerge as leaders in their adult life.

Studying 60 babies with brain damage and their normal counterparts, Dr. Samuel

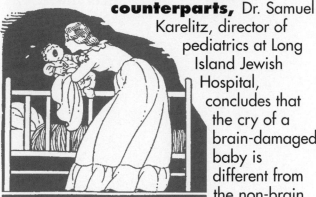

Karelitz, director of pediatrics at Long Island Jewish Hospital, concludes that the cry of a brain-damaged baby is different from the non-brain damaged children in that they don't cry as quickly when stimulated to do so and their cry is spasmodic and irregular.

WHO WEARS THE PANTS IN YOUR FAMILY?

Studies conducted at McGill University indicate children who grow up in homes where the fathers are dominant tend to be more emotionally well-adjusted than those where mothers are the bosses.

Babies born to drug-addicted mothers

can be addicts themselves and have a lower chance for survival unless diagnosed and treated immediately.

MUSIC DOTH SOOTHE THE SAVAGE CHILD

8-Year Old Disturbed Youngsters Calm Down Considerably When Soft, Classical Music Is Played In The Classroom According To Tests Conducted By Professor Charles H. Patterson, Jr, Of Longwood College, Farmville, Virginia.

Today's Health magazine reports that despite medical advances, old wives tales regarding pregnancy still exist such as **if you wear high heels your baby will be cross-eyed** or **if you go out in the rain, the baby will drown** or **if you have heart-burn your baby will be hairy.**

- New Jersey's 90-Year Old Statute Limiting The Sale Of Contraceptives Is Held Unconstitutional.

- Ground Breaking Research Being Conducted At Stanford Medical Center Gives New Hope To Women Unable To Bear Children Through A New Process Of Fertilization In Which Fertilized Donor Eggs Are Implanted Surgically.

NOBEL PRIZES

MEDICINE & PHYSIOLOGY	PHYSICS	CHEMISTRY
Severo Ochoa (U. S.) and Arthur Kornberg (U. S.)	Emilio G. Segré (U. S.) and Owen Chamberlain (U. S.)	Jaroslav Heyrovsky (Czechoslovakia)

THE AMA APPROVES HYPNOSIS AS A MEDICAL AID IF ADMINISTERED BY TRAINED PHYSICIANS OR DENTISTS.

DR. A. H. C. SINCLAIR-GIEBEN OF THE UNIVERSITY OF ABERDEEN, SCOTLAND REPORTS EXCELLENT SUCCESS IN TREATING PATIENTS WITH WARTS THROUGH THE USE OF HYPNOSIS CITING 10 OUT OF 14 CASES WHERE THE WARTS DISAPPEARED FROM THE "TREATED" HANDS.

The Army Quartermasters Corp. is testing a line of disposable hospital paper products including nightgowns, sheets and gowns for doctors and nurses.

Hospital staph infections cause great alarm in the medical world as infections sweep through hospitals from nurseries to wards causing deaths.

GOLF WIDOWS SHOULD REJOICE
Men who play golf have lower risk of heart attacks and are generally easier to live with.

$250,000 is allocated by the U. S. Public Health Service for the study of the smog problem in Los Angeles.

SOME LIKE IT HOT OR EVEN HOTTER
Scientific research being conducted at Rutgers University on mosquitoes seems to indicate that they target their meals based on their potential meals' body heat and it seems that skinny people are more appetizing than the fatter ones.

LOVE & MARRIAGE DON'T GO TOGETHER LIKE THE HORSE & CARRIAGE

New York University anthropologist Professor Ernest Van Den Haag contends that since love is by its nature irrational, unpredictable and frenzied it should not be a major component in deciding who should be your mate as evidenced by the high divorce rate in the U. S.

According to a joint study conducted by Drs. James B. Hamilton and Gordon E. Mestler, State University of New York and Harumi Terada, Tokyo University, Caucasian women tend to have more facial hair than their Japanese counterparts and older white women tend to grow mustaches, especially if they're French.

Severely depressed women at California's Camarillo State Hospital being given beauty treatments to try to rebuild their self-esteem.

Even though the hormone dramatically relieves symptoms, doctors are hesitant to give menopausal women estrogen because of their concern that it could possibly cause cancer although no definitive research backs up their fear.

Two out of three doctors are women in the Soviet Union.

INTERNATIONAL
presents
Two New Furniture Groupings
by BRIAN

For the name of your dealer, write
INTERNATIONAL FURNITURE • Division of Schnadig Corporation
4820 West Belmont Avenue • Chicago 41, Illinois

**A world of comfort . . . whichever way you lean . . .
to the latest in modern . . . or to the charm of Early American**

MODERN AMERICA by BRIAN (above) . . . every line a stroke of ingenious design. Narrow of arm, deep of seat. Foam rubber filled. Textured strié cover in turquoise, apricot, charcoal brown, natural, beige, cocoa brown.

Ten go-together pieces to choose from: Shown: One-armed Sofa, $189.50; Curved Corner Section, $119.50; Right Bumper Section, $139.50; Extension Ottoman, $54.00. Not shown: Over-size Sofa, $199.50; Lounge Chair, $99.50; Left and Right Arm Sections, $119.50 each; Left Bumper Section, $139.50; Armless Chair, $59.50. Prices slightly higher west of the Rockies.

AMERICAN SETTLER by BRIAN (below) . . . authentic Early American in design, but very up-to-date in the way it functions in your home. Rubbed maple finish. Covered in tweed (brown, beige, turquoise, gold, spice) or Colonial tapestry (natural with brown, gold, terra cotta, or toast color).

Shown: Winged Sofa, $189.50; Winged Chair, $119.50. Also available: Swivel Rocker Chair, $69.50; Left or Right Arm Winged Section, $119.50 each; Curved Corner Section, $119.50. Dav-N-Bed also available. Slightly higher in foam. Prices slightly higher west of the Rockies.

NEW PRODUCTS AND INVENTIONS

HERBERT, ARE YOU AWAKE AND SITTING?

Simmons Co. Develops A Bed That Wakes You By Bringing The Bed Up To A Sitting Position.

The First American Made Alarm Wristwatch Goes On Sale By General Time Corp.'s Westclox.

You Can Get A New Electric Timer That Plugs Into Any Of Your Household Appliances From Mrs. Dorothy Damar Of Elizabeth, N. J.

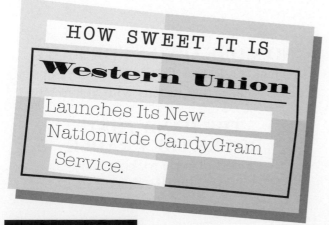

HOW SWEET IT IS

Western Union Launches Its New Nationwide CandyGram Service.

A CHILLING EXPERIENCE

Bartenders Can Now Give You As Many Chilled And Frosted Glasses As You Like Thanks To A New Device Called "Frosty-Glass."

A DISPOSABLE TOOTHBRUSH PRE-FILLED WITH TOOTHPASTE IS INTRODUCED BY THE FLEX-I-BRUSH CORP. OF LODI, NEW JERSEY.

A PAPER DOLL NO MORE

The First **BARBIE DOLL** With Clothes Made Of Real Fabric Hits The Market.

HOOVER GETS READY TO MARKET A LIGHTWEIGHT ELECTRIC FLOOR WASHER THAT SCRUBS THEN DRIES FLOORS.

Say The Magic Woid And You Get Instant Eyebrows

Elizabeth Arden sells new false eyebrows made of human hair which are applied to the skin with surgical glue.

WATCH FOR THE FALL-OUT

From Charmfit of Hollywood the first bra with a Velcro closing is now available.

The New Zip Master will help women zip up those hard to reach back zippers through the use of this handy new product.

AUTOMATION COMES TO THE POST OFFICE

Pitney-Bowes invents an automatic cancelling machine, being installed in post offices around the country, that can process up to 27,000 letters an hour vs. the current 16,000 per hour.

Vending machines that dispense stamps, paper and envelopes will soon be hitting your local post office.

A portable, fully transistorized tape recorder weighing in at three pounds is available from the Mohawk Business Machines Co. of Brooklyn, New York.

GETTING ALL CHARGED UP

Look for the new line of rechargeable batteries with a 15-20 year life expectancy to be in your stores soon.

Cows Who Have Chewed Away Their Front Teeth Can Now Be Fitted With False Teeth Invented By A Colorado Rancher And A Dentist From Nebraska.

Xerox Is Working On A Tabletop Machine That Will Copy Documents On Untreated Paper.

Reynolds Metals Co. Introduces Its Aluminum Roof Shingles Carrying A Lifetime Guarantee.

A Small Oxygen Cannister Is Available For Emergency Home Treatment For Cardiac Arrest.

NO MORE OWIES FOR BABY

Manhattan's Riegel Textile Corp. develops a pinless diaper that fastens with Velcro tabs.

THE HAND THAT ROCKS THE CRADLE

A new electric rocking baby cradle hits the market.

WHAT A YEAR IT WAS!

READY FOR YOUR CLOSE-UP?

Zoomar, Inc. of Glen Cove, New York develops a new lens that can shoot both close ups and long shots.

A 3" pocket size 8mm camera is being marketed by Bolsey-Delmonico of Long Island City, New York.

LET'S NOT MAKE LIGHT OF THIS

The world's smallest flash bulb—fitting into the palm of a hand—is being manufactured by General Electric.

Revere Flash-Matic develops a flash gun which holds six bulbs.

SMILE, YOU'RE ON CAMERA

Mosler Safe Co. develops a surveillance system for banks that uses a motion picture camera.

SMILE EARTHLING

RCA develops electrostatic photography process which some day could allow the earth to be photographed from outer space.

WHAT A YEAR IT WAS!

You Light Up My Time

A new lamp that both lights up and gives you the time is being sold for $19.95-$39.95 by a Milwaukee company.

Now You Can See What You're Writing

A combination ballpoint pen and flashlight, developed in West Germany and sold in the U. S. by Chicago's Crittenton Manufacturing Co. is priced at $4.95.

Hats That Go Flash In The Night

Clever Things, Inc. of Cincinnati, Ohio develops a beanie cap with built-in battery-operated flashing beacon light.

AND NOW, CUSTOM MUSIC FOR YOUR FACTORIES AND OFFICES

A Chicago company is selling a small record player capable of playing 1,000 songs on up to 25 records.

MUSIC TO YOUR EARS

Thanks to Lafayette Radio, Jamaica, New York, you can now have music piped directly into your ears through a resistor radio built into your sunglasses.

RCA develops new anti-static record that resists dust and lint.

THE MUSIC GOES ROUND AND ROUND AND COMES OUT WHERE?

A chair with built-in speakers for your listening pleasure has hit the market from $159.

HAVE TELEVISION, WILL TRAVEL

A compact 15 lb. portable television is being sold by Philco Corp. at around $250.

HI HONEY...WHOOPS I MEAN HELLO SIR!

AT&T develops the call director, a new 18-button phone capable of receiving multiple calls through an illuminated push-button panel, allowing calls to be placed on hold while another call is answered. It's also an intercom system for up to 29 office extensions.

Two Belgian inventors develop Teledial, a gadget that recalls and automatically dials phone numbers.

RCA develops a small radio phone the size of a shoe box and weighing less than 10 pounds.

THE GIFT OF SPEECH

Bell Telephone invents a transistorized artificial larynx allowing people with damaged vocal cords to speak.

Bell Telephone Laboratories is assigned patent of inventor Floyd F. Becker of Summit, New Jersey for his television telephone invention.

DIALING IN THE DARK

A new telephone which has the dial in an illuminated handpiece, is being tested in the New Jersey area by the Bell Telephone Co.

WALK, WALKED... DONE WALKED

Karl A. Pansch Develops A Machine That Helps Students Conjugate Irregular English Verbs.

29-Year Old MIT Researcher, Douglas T. Ross, Develops Mechanical Brain With 107-Word Vocabulary For Use In Automation.

Called The Beginning Of The Second Industrial Revolution, RCA And The Army Signal Corps Develop A Micromodule Which Will Greatly Reduce Electronic Products As 27 Of These Chips Can Be Placed In Only One Cubic Inch Of Space.

Tidewater Oil Comes Up With A New Gasoline Which They Claim Causes Less Pollution.

An Electronic Addition To Vending Machines Gives Change After Purchases.

Electronic Banking Begins In California.

A remote-controlled typewriter designed for paralyzed people who operate the machine through their head and neck muscles is developed.

The Federal Communications Commission grants permission for private citizens to have two-way radios creating the Citizen Radio Service providing 22 radio channels.

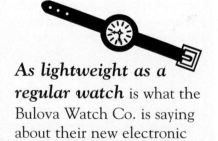

As lightweight as a regular watch is what the Bulova Watch Co. is saying about their new electronic wristwatch.

WHAT A YEAR IT WAS!

SUGAR & MILK FOR BREAKFAST

Frosty O's, General Mills' New Breakfast Cereal, Is Showing Up In Breakfast Bowls Across The Country.

New Streamlined One-Piece Packaging Is Developed For Frozen Foods Replacing The Bulky Double Package.

ATTENTION SHOPPERS: SPECIAL TODAY...

"Store Video," A Closed-Circuit In-House Advertising Tool For Supermarkets Will Soon Be In Your Favorite A & P.

Westinghouse Designs The Dog-O-Matic—

An Appliance That Can Cook Six Frankfurters In Just 90 Seconds.

Metrecal Diet Drink *Introduced By The Mead Johnson Co. Is A Hit.*

JUST FOLLOW THAT YELLOW LINE

Minnesota Mining & Manufacturing develops an illuminating paint for airport runways and taxi strips.

SAN FRANCISCO INTERNATIONAL AIRPORT

initiates use of first "Jetwalk" in the nation developed to protect passengers from weather conditions by allowing them to board airplanes through a telescoping indoor corridor.

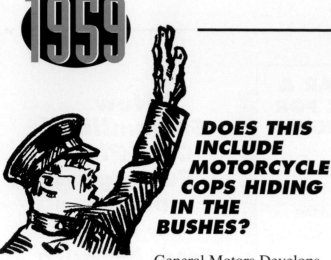

1959

DOES THIS INCLUDE MOTORCYCLE COPS HIDING IN THE BUSHES?

General Motors Develops Experimental Car Equipped With Radar Equipment To Warn Drivers Of Road Hazards.

A New Speed-Control Device For Highway Driving Is Developed By The Glide Control Corporation Of Inglewood, California.

IF I COULD ONLY FIND THE KNOB ON THIS FA-SCHUNKT-KANER MACHINE

Facing Loss Of Their Licenses For At Least Five Years For Drunken Driving, Germans Take Advantage Of A New Machine At Their Neighborhood Tavern Which For Only 50 Pfennigs ($ .12 U. S.) Measures The Blood Alcohol Level.

Chevrolet Corvair Becomes First American Car With Engine In The Rear.

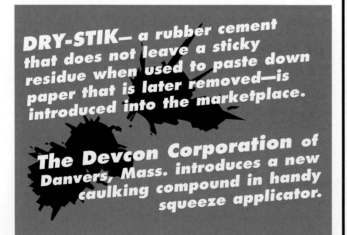

DRY-STIK— a rubber cement that does not leave a sticky residue when used to paste down paper that is later removed—is introduced into the marketplace.

The Devcon Corporation of Danvers, Mass. introduces a new caulking compound in handy squeeze applicator.

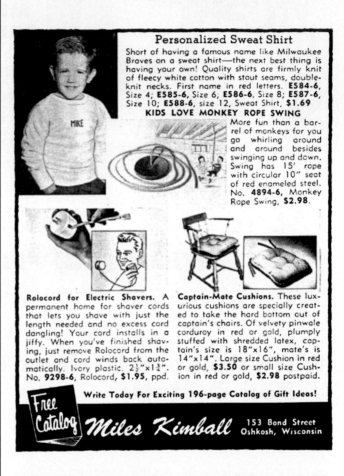

WHAT A YEAR IT WAS!

It's A **Wright, Wright, Wright** World

Despite his death on April 9, numerous FRANK LLOYD WRIGHT projects garner attention throughout the year.

Models of well-known buildings can be seen when "Form Givers At Mid-Century" opens at the Corcoran Gallery in Washington D.C. Represented architects include Frank Lloyd Wright, Eero Saarinen, Ludwig Mies van der Rohe, and Le Corbusier.

Harvard's Walter Gropius receives the American Institute of Architects' gold medal.

Winners of the American Institute of Architects' Honor Awards include I.M. Pei & Associates and Eero Saarinen & Associates.

San Francisco's Crown Zellerbach and John Hancock buildings, designed by famed architectural firm Skidmore, Owings & Merrill are completed, beginning the revitalization of the Market Street area.

OCTOBER SEES THE GRAND OPENING of the ultra-modern, cylindrical Solomon R. Guggenheim Museum *(above)*, the only Wright structure in Manhattan. It is by far the grandest gallery for non-objective art in the world.

HIS BETH SHALOM SYNAGOGUE in Elkins Park, Pennsylvania, opens.

PATTERNED FABRICS for home use designed by Wright are available.

PASSINGS

Architect's architect **FRANK LLOYD WRIGHT**, whose designs revolutionized the architecture field and who incorporated the surrounding natural elements into his designs, is dead at age 89. Famous throughout the world, his structures dot landscapes as far away as Tokyo and as close as his own home, "Taliesin," in Wisconsin.

1959

$11,750 buys a three bedroom, two bathroom house with a swimming pool near Phoenix, Arizona. Down payment is approximately $400.

Nearly 50,000 pools are built in backyards across the country, many for middle-class families.

Key words in home furnishings include
walnut
grace
modern
affordable
traditional
shelves
pattern
skylights
vinyl
wallpaper
lengthy

Brown, blue, green, orange and **yellow** are some of the year's favorite decorating colors.

Construction for the first completely automated post office in the U. S. begins in Providence, Rhode Island.

A gigantic aluminum frame structure named *"Octet Truss,"* designed by R. Buckminster Fuller, can be seen in New York at the Museum of Modern Art.

R. Buckminster Fuller's gold geodesic dome houses the entire United States Exhibition in Moscow.

Designer **Charles Eames** produces a documentary for the United States Exhibition which shows the Russian people different aspects of life in America.

Ground is broken in London for what is to be the highest office building in Great Britain.

Looking like an enormous martini glass, a water tower is built in Helsinki, Finland.

FRANCE

Imminent destruction of a **Le Corbusier** designed home outside of Paris causes an outcry from architects around the world.

•

An underground church is built in Lourdes.

•

Le Corbusier finishes Convent La Tourette near Lyons.

movies

"The Diary Of Anne Frank,"

A Riveting Drama Of A Jewish Family's Ordeal In Amsterdam During World War II, Leaves Audiences Stunned.

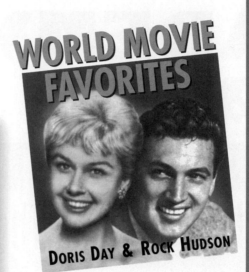

WORLD MOVIE FAVORITES

DORIS DAY & ROCK HUDSON

TONIGHT AT 8:30

GEORGE STEVENS'

THE DIARY OF ANNE FRANK

CinemaScope
Stereophonic Sound
20
AIR CONDITIONED

RKO·PALACE
B WAY & 47th ST. PL7·2626

Tickets Available at Box·Office

DISNEY

Walt Disney's 7-years-in-the-making "Sleeping Beauty" fails to recoup its production cost of six million dollars.

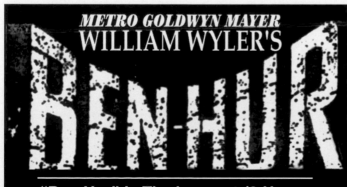

METRO GOLDWYN MAYER
WILLIAM WYLER'S
BEN-HUR

"Ben Hur" Is The Longest (3 Hours, 50 Minutes) And Costliest American Film Ever Made With A Budget Of $15 Million And Reserved Seats Going For A Top Price Of $4.00.

1959

31 Thirty-First
ACADEMY AWARDS PRESENTATION
Held At The Pantages Theatre.

Tony Curtis and **Janet Leigh** among the hundreds of stars and luminaries present to honor Hollywood's finest.

RKO
PANTAGES
31ST ANNUAL
ACADEMY AWARDS PRESENTATIONS
THE ACADEMY OF MOTION PICTURE ARTS AND SCIENCES

31ST Annual ACADEMY AWARDS

WHAT A YEAR IT WAS!

Returning to Hollywood after a 10-year absence, **Ingrid Bergman** attracts an extra measure of attention from the excited fans.

With Glamorous Kim Novak Looking On, James Cagney Is About To Announce The Academy's Choice For Best Actress Of The Year.

After being nominated four times, Susan Hayward finally receives an Oscar for her performance in "I Want To Live" which is presented to her by Miss Novak.

As John Wayne looks on, David Niven receives a kiss and best actor award from Irene Dunne for his performance in "Separate Tables."

"And The Winner Is..."

BEST PICTURE
Gigi

BEST ACTOR
DAVID NIVEN, *Separate Tables*

BEST ACTRESS
SUSAN HAYWARD, *I Want To Live!*

BEST DIRECTOR
VINCENTE MINNELLI, *Gigi*

BEST SUPPORTING ACTOR
BURL IVES, *The Big Country*

BEST SUPPORTING ACTRESS
WENDY HILLER, *Separate Tables*

BEST SONG
"GIGI," *Gigi*

Academy Award Champ.
9 Awards
"Best Picture"
GiGi M·G·M

1959 Favorites
(Oscars Presented In 1960)

Charlton Heston

BEST PICTURE
BEN-HUR

BEST ACTOR
CHARLTON HESTON, *BEN-HUR*

BEST ACTRESS
SIMONE SIGNORET, *Room At The Top*

BEST DIRECTOR
WILLIAM WYLER, *BEN-HUR*

BEST SUPPORTING ACTOR
HUGH GRIFFITH, *BEN-HUR*

Simone Signoret

BEST SUPPORTING ACTRESS
SHELLEY WINTERS, *The Diary Of Anne Frank*

BEST SONG
"HIGH HOPES," *A Hole In The Head*

WHAT A YEAR IT WAS!

AUDREY HEPBURN
Wins Best Actress Nod From The New York Film Critics' Circle For Her Work In

the nun's story.

Alfred Hitchcock's
"North By Northwest"
Sets Non-Holiday Two-Week Box Office Record At New York's Radio City Music Hall Raking In A Cool $404,056.

"ONE OF THE YEAR'S MOST HONEST, AFFECTING AND FINEST DRAMAS!"
—A. H. WEILER, *TIMES*

FRANCOIS TRUFFAUT
Named Best Director At The

cannes film festival

For
"The 400 Blows."

"ROOM AT THE TOP"
Starring
LAURENCE HARVEY • HEATHER SEARS • SIMONE SIGNORET
Relulus Films Ltd. Production • A Continental Distributing, Inc. Release

FINE ARTS
58th Street bet. Park & Lex. • PLaza 5-6030
Feature at: 12, 2, 4, 6, 8 and 10

Hailed by the British Film Academy As The Best Film Of The Year, Simone Signoret Gives An Extraordinary Performance As The Older Woman Having An Affair With The Unscrupulous Younger Man, Laurence Harvey, In "Room At The Top."

Famous Births

Tom Arnold	Bronson Pinchot
Rupert Everett	Aidan Quinn
Val Kilmer	Kevin Spacey
Matthew Modine	Emma Thompson

1001 Arabian Nights
The 400 Blows
A Hole In The Head
AL CAPONE
ALASKA PASSAGE
Alias Jesse James
Anatomy Of A Murder
The Angry Red Planet
Aparajito
The Beat Generation
Beloved Infidel
Ben-Hur
The Big Circus
The Big Fisherman
BLACK ORCHID
BLACK ORPHEUS
The Blue Angel

Blue Denim
Breathless
Carry On Sargeant
CASPER'S BIRTHDAY PARTY
Cast A Long Shadow
COMPULSION
Crime & Punishment, USA
Day Of The Outlaw
The Diary Of Anne Frank
THE FBI STORY
The Fugitive Kind
The Gene Krupa Story
GIDGET
HERCULES
Hiroshima, Mon Amour
THE HORSE SOLDIERS
The Hound Of The Baskervilles
Imitation Of Life
Journey To The Center Of The Earth
La Dolce Vita
The Last Angry Man
The Legend Of Tom Dooley

GREGORY PECK — PORK CHOP HILL

"POWERFUL AND SHATTERING!" —Cue Magazine

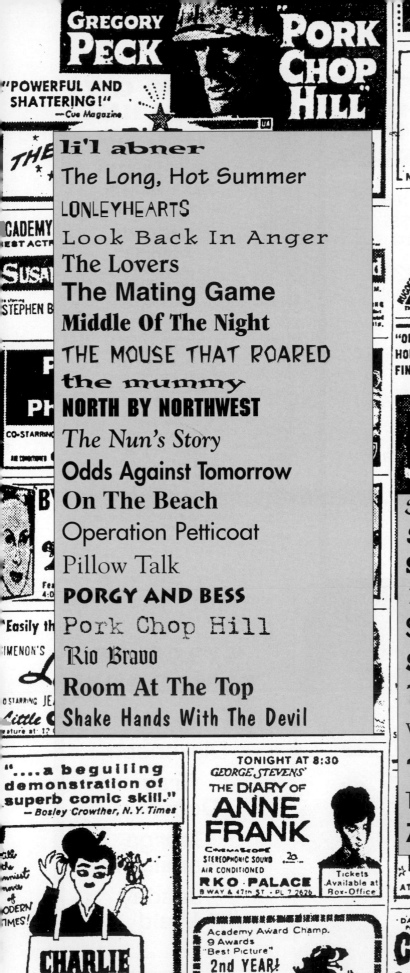

li'l abner
The Long, Hot Summer
LONLEYHEARTS
Look Back In Anger
The Lovers
The Mating Game
Middle Of The Night
THE MOUSE THAT ROARED
the mummy
NORTH BY NORTHWEST
The Nun's Story
Odds Against Tomorrow
On The Beach
Operation Petticoat
Pillow Talk
PORGY AND BESS
Pork Chop Hill
Rio Bravo
Room At The Top
Shake Hands With The Devil

Strindberg's of LOVE and LUST
"The best production, direction, photography and performances we've had from Sweden" —Jesse Zunser, Cue
starring MAI ZETTERLING and ANITA BJORK
AIR-CONDITIONED BEEKMAN 65th St. at 2nd

EXTENDED AMERICAN PREMIERE
Jules Dassin's Masterpiece "HE WHO MUST DIE"
ART 8th ST. E. of 5th AVE.
GRAMERCY E. 23rd ST. at LEX. AVE.
8th STREET EAST of 6th AVE.
"Why Quibble?—Perfect!" —N.Y. Times
FERNANDEL in "FORBIDDEN FRUIT"
with Francoise Arnoul
plus Academy Award Winner "The RED BALLOON"

"ONE OF THE YEAR'S MOST HONEST, AFFECTING AND FINEST DRAMAS!" —A. H. WEILER, TIMES

LAS 4 DAY.
lon chaney sr.
in his most memorable ro...
'THE PHANTOM OF THE OPERA'
(Full-length feature with live piano ...nt)
10:40, plus

Sleeping Beauty
Some Came Running
Some Like It Hot
The Sound And The Fury
Strangers When We Meet
Suddenly, Last Summer
Tarzan, The Ape Man
Wild Strawberries
The Wreck Of Mary Deare
The Young Philadelphians
Zorro Rides Again

"....a beguiling demonstration of superb comic skill." —Bosley Crowther, N.Y. Times

CHARLIE CHAPLIN MODERN

TONIGHT AT 8:30
GEORGE STEVENS'
THE DIARY OF ANNE FRANK
CINEMASCOPE
STEREOPHONIC SOUND
AIR CONDITIONED
RKO PALACE
B'WAY & 47th ST · PL 7 2626
Tickets Available at Box-Office

Academy Award Champ.
9 Awards 'Best Picture'
2nd YEAR!
SUTTON
EAST 57th STREET

HEAVEN Guild 50s
33 West 50th St. at Rockefeller Pl. · PL 7-7406 7
AT: 11, 12:30, 2:15, 4:05, 6:25, 8:15, 10:10
EXTRA! in color! "MONTAUK"

DARRYL F. ZANUCK Productions, Inc. presents
COMPULSION
CINEMASCOPE
In the Wonder of HIGH-FIDELITY STEREOPHONIC SOUND
Doors Open 10:00 A.M.
Rivoli B'way & 49th St.
CONTINUOUS PERFORMANCES
"A GREAT WORK

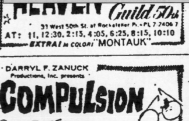

CHARLIE CHAPLIN 'THE GOLD RUSH'
AIR COND. 86 St. Bet. Lex. & 3rd Ave.
GRANDE AT 9-7720

113

1959

★ New Crop Of HOLLYWOOD ACTRESSSES

Shirley MacLaine

Shirley MacLaine, *25*
*Hottest Actress
In Hollywood*

May Britt, *23*
("The Young Lions")

Lee Remick, *23*
("Face In The Crowd," "The Long, Hot Summer")

Carolyn Jones, *26*
("Marjorie Morningstar," "A Hole In The Head")

Susan Kohner, *22*
("To Hell And Back," "The Big Fisherman")

Diane Baker, *21*
("The Diary Of Anne Frank")

★ **Hope Lange**, *24*
("Bus Stop," "Peyton Place")

STARS WHO BRING IN BIG BUCKS AT THE BOX OFFICE

Doris Day
Glenn Ford
Cary Grant
Susan Hayward
Rock Hudson
Jerry Lewis
Debbie Reynolds
Frank Sinatra
James Stewart
John Wayne

Cary Grant

John Wayne

STARS OF TOMORROW

★ Angie Dickenson

Troy Donahue

George Hamilton

★ Tuesday Weld

114

WHAT A YEAR IT WAS!

VARIETY ▪ CLUBS INTERNATIONAL

sends a delegation, including Kim Novak and Perry Como, to visit President Eisenhower to mark the Club's 32nd year.

Ike joins 10,000 from show business who combine forces to aid their needy, raising over $75,000,000 through the years.

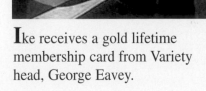

Ike receives a gold lifetime membership card from Variety head, George Eavey.

"PILLOW

ROCK HUDSON DORIS DAY "PILLOW TALK"

TONY RANDALL • THELMA RITTER

Among the luminaries attending the East Coast Palace Premier are Ross Hunter *(top)* and U.I. President Milton Rackmil and his wife, Vivian Blaine *(bottom).*

New York's finest *(above)* hold back the enthusiastic crowd as they strain to get a look at the film's star Rock Hudson who arrives with Tallulah Bankhead *(right).*

WHAT A YEAR IT WAS!

TALK"
Has Gala East Coast And West Coast Premiers

RKO PALACE

Sharing in the ovation is the ever-popular Thelma Ritter, another of Pillow Talk's comedy stars.

Meanwhile, Downtown, The New Murray Hill Theatre Is The Site Of Yet Another Showing Of "Pillow Talk" With Fire Commissioner Kavanagh Wielding The Axe To Officially Open The Theatre.

Novelist Patty Hurst (*top*), socialite Hope Hampton (*center*) and actor Tony Randall (*bottom*) all attend this gala benefit for the United Nations School.

1959

meanwhile... on the

Esther Williams and Jeff Chandler attend the premiere.

Rock Hudson just arrives by plane from New York for the debut of the comedy success.

Completing the picture is Doris Day, herself, "Pillow Talk's" leading lady and America's #1 film star.

WEST COAST

INVITATIONAL PREMIERE

PILLOW TALK

1959

THE HARVARD LAMPOON

PLEASE DON'T OPEN THE ENVELOPE

Kirk Douglas' performance in "The Vikings" wins him the not so coveted Harvard Lampoon's Worst Actor Of The Year Award for the third time.

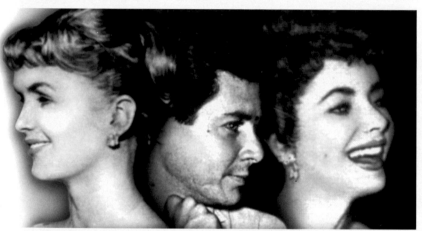

...for the most entertaining off-screen performances, The Harvard Lampoon gives a special award to **Elizabeth Taylor**, **Debbie Reynolds** and **Eddie Fisher** for their marriage go round.

AhEAd BY a NOSe

Theater owner Walter Reade, Jr. announces the premiere of an odoriferous film, nosing out Mike Todd, Jr.'s premiere of "Smell-O-Vision," a process developed for pumping a variety of odors into movie theaters.

Gregory Peck Declines Co-Starring Role With Marilyn Monroe In "Let's Make Love" Because The Parts Are Not Evenly Developed.

To escape the mob Tony Curtis and Jack Lemmon put on dresses in **"SOME LIKE IT HOT"** and join an all-girl band with Marilyn Monroe singing vocals.

WHAT A YEAR IT WAS!

Frank Capra Casts **Frank Sinatra** In "**A Hole In The Head.**"

ROD STEIGER'S AL CAPONE PRECIPITATES A RASH OF GANGSTER FILMS.

YUL BRYNNER (TOP) **Takes Over Role In "Solomon and Sheba" After The Untimely Death Of TYRONE POWER Last Year.**

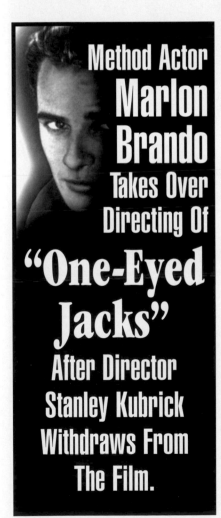

Method Actor **Marlon Brando** Takes Over Directing Of "**One-Eyed Jacks**" After Director Stanley Kubrick Withdraws From The Film.

PASSINGS

Star of the renowned film "**THE INFORMER,**" for which he won an Oscar, actor Victor McLaglen, former wrestler, policeman and gold prospector, dies at age 72.

Charles Vidor, who directed "**HANS CHRISTIAN ANDERSEN**" and "**A SONG TO REMEMBER**" dies at age 58 of a heart attack in Vienna.

Theatre, movie, radio and television star Paul Douglas, whose performance in the long-running "**BORN YESTERDAY**" on Broadway brought him fame, dies of a heart attack at age 52.

Swashbuckling movie star Errol Flynn, whose adventures off-screen rivaled those he had in "**ROBIN HOOD,**" "**ADVENTURES OF DON JUAN**" and "**CAPTAIN BLOOD,**" dies at age 50.

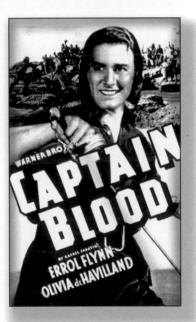

One of the first and greatest movie moguls, producer, director and film pioneer Cecil B. DeMille, whose movies read like a greatest hits of the bible ("**THE TEN COMMANDMENTS,**" "**SAMSON AND DELILAH,**" "**KING OF KINGS**"), dies of a heart attack at age 77.

Best known for his Oscar winning role of Santa Claus in the classic "**MIRACLE ON 34TH STREET,**" actor Edmund Gwenn dies at age 81.

When your TV picture tube needs replacing, remember this...

NOW...AN RCA PICTURE TUBE TO FIT EVERY BUDGET!

All-New Premium

RCA Silverama®

Finest Picture Tube Made Today!

Factory-Rebuilt

RCA Monogram

No Finer Rebuilt Picture Tube Made!

Not just one RCA television picture tube...but a choice of two!

When the picture on your TV fades, dulls or blacks out—when your TV technician tells you the picture tube should be replaced, remember you now have a choice of two kinds of RCA picture tubes:

• **RCA SILVERAMA**—A premium picture tube—constructed of all-new glass and parts. Made for the TV viewer who wants the finest picture his set can deliver.

• **RCA MONOGRAM**—A rebuilt picture tube of dependable quality for the budget-minded. Reprocessed and tested in the same factory as RCA's premium picture tubes.

Both RCA SILVERAMA and RCA MONOGRAM are warranted for one full year...and there's a size to fit virtually every make and model TV set. Your local TV service technician can give you complete information and prices. Remember: for the best in television be sure to say...RCA.

 **RADIO CORPORATION OF AMERICA**

Electron Tube Division • Harrison, N. J.

What is a picture tube?

The picture tube — in simple terms — is actually a glass or metal bulb containing a "gun" which emits a stream of electrons. These electrons strike a layer of phosphor on the inside surface of the glass face —causing the phosphor to "glow", thus "painting" a TV picture on the face of the tube.

Two kinds of tubes

There are two kinds of picture tubes—new tubes constructed of all-new materials and parts, and also picture tubes known as "rebuilts". A "rebuilt" is simply a used picture tube that has been repaired by replacing the gun and possibly the phosphor and then reprocessed.

Actually, there's nothing wrong with "rebuilts". Retread tires and many other reconditioned devices can give you satisfactory performance. But the quality of most rebuilt products is limited by the rebuilder's skill and know-how. With a rebuilt picture tube the big question is—will it provide you with the bright, sharp picture you want for greater TV enjoyment? Now you *can* be sure! There is no finer rebuilt picture tube made than the RCA MONOGRAM.

So now you have a choice in RCA picture tubes:

• **RCA Silverama**...A premium picture tube—made of all-new glass and all-new parts.

• **RCA Monogram**...No finer factory-rebuilt picture tube made.

TELEVISION

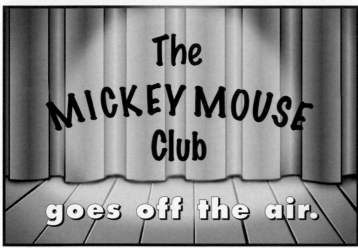

The **MICKEY MOUSE** Club **goes off the air.**

SO LONG FOR A WHILE

The long-running *"Your Hit Parade"* goes off the air.

CBS announces that **Edward R. Murrow** is taking a leave of absence for a year.

STEVE ALLEN

slaps a cease and desist warning on **Greyhound Bus Lines** from using the name **"Steverino"** for their dog after they terminate sponsorship of Allen's show.

Rod Serling's

TWILIGHT ZONE

makes its television debut, taking viewers into a new world called **"The Sixth Dimension."**

Also Premiering
Five Fingers
Mr. Lucky
Peck's Bad Girl
Wichita Town
Pete Kelly's Blues

WHAT A YEAR IT WAS!

POPULAR

90% of American homes have television sets cutting into movie attendance.

77 Sunset Strip

Adventures In Paradise

The Alaskans

Alcoa Presents

Alfred Hitchcock Presents

The Andy Williams Show

The Ann Sothern Show

Bachelor Father

Bat Masterson

The Betty Hutton Show

Black Saddle

Blondie

Bold Journey

Bold Venture

Bonanza

Bourbon Street Beat

Broken Arrow

Bronco

Buckskin

Californians

Cheyenne

Colt .45

Concentration

The Danny Thomas Show

Andy Williams

Alfred Hitchcock

Betty Hutton

Lucille Ball

The David Niven Show

December Bride

The Dennis O'Keefe Show

Dennis The Menace

The Deputy

The Dick Clark Show

The Donna Reed Show

Dragnet

The Ed Sullivan Show

Fibber McGee and Molly

Gunsmoke

Have Gun Will Travel

Hawaiian Eye

I Love Lucy

I've Got A Secret

The Invisible Man

The Jack Benny Show

The Jack Paar Show

The Jackie Gleason Show

The Jimmie Rodgers Show

John Gunther's High Road

The Joseph Cotton Show

A HORSE OF ANOTHER COLOR

Bonanza

is first western to be broadcast in color.

Jack Benny

Lassie

Phil Silvers

Walter Winchell

Kraft Music Hall Presents: The Dave King Show

Laramie

Lassie

The Lawrence Welk Show

Leave It To Beaver

The Life And Legend Of Wyatt Earp

The Loretta Young Show

Love And Marriage

M Squad

Manhunt

The Many Loves Of Dobie Gillis

Maverick

Men Into Space

The Millionaire

Music For A Summer Night

Naked City

Name That Tune

Northwest Passage

Perry Mason

Peter Gunn

The Phil Silvers Show

Philip Marlowe

The Price Is Right

Rawhide

The Real McCoys

The Rebel

The Red Skelton Show

The Rifleman

Riverboat

Rocky And His Friends

The Rough Riders

Shirley Temple's Storybook

The Spike Jones Show

Startime

Steve Canyon

Tales Of Wells Fargo

The Thin Man

Tightrope

Trackdown

The Twilight Zone

The Untouchables

Wagon Train

The Walter Winchell Show

Wanted: Dead Or Alive

Westinghouse Desilu Playhouse

All This And Uncle Miltie Too

Euripides' Medea starring **Judith Anderson** kicks off New York's maverick WNTA-TV's new *"The Play Of The Week"* series followed by Ivan Turgenev's A Month In The Country starring **Uta Hagen, Luther Adler** and **Alexander Scourby**.

Judith Anderson

Vivien Leigh makes her British television debut playing Sabrina in Thornton Wilder's The Skin Of Our Teeth.

16-year old beauty **Tuesday Weld** appears on CBS-TV's new teen television comedy THE MANY LOVES OF DOBIE GILLIS.

That's A Lot Of Velveeta

Singer **Perry Como** signs two-year, $25 million contract with Kraft Foods Company to produce 104 weekly one-hour shows with Como starring in a little less than half of them.

A viewing audience of eight million tune into NBC's production of **Gian-Carlo Menotti's** opera, Maria Golovin.

The television production of W. Somerset Maugham's The Moon And Sixpence garners **Sir Laurence Olivier** critical acclaim.

NBC's new team— **Chet Huntley** and **David Brinkley** garner awards for their in-depth news coverage and commentaries.

WHAT A YEAR IT WAS!

Emmy Awards

Series:

Dramatic: **Playhouse 90**

Comedy: **The Jack Benny Show**

Musical: **The Dinah Shore Chevy Show**

Western: **Maverick**

Performers:

Drama: **Loretta Young** The Loretta Young Show

Raymond Burr Perry Mason

Comedy: **Jane Wyatt** Father Knows Best

Jack Benny The Jack Benny Show

Fred Astaire's television special is nominated for, and wins, **nine Emmys** including **Actor, Program** and **Director.**

Famous Births

Jason **ALEXANDER**
Danny **BONADUCE**
Judd **NELSON**
Mackenzie **PHILLIPS**
David **HYDE PIERCE**
Jean **SMART**
Tracey **ULLMAN**

WHAT A YEAR IT WAS!

1959
ADVERTISEMENT

127

AND NOW FOR ALL YOU NUTS OUT THERE, AN INSTANT SOLUTION TO YOUR PROBLEMS

31-year old blonde psychologist **Joyce Brothers** gets late-night television psychiatry slot—"Consult Dr. Brothers"—following "The Jack Paar Show."

The Peter Tchaikovsky Story,

presented by **"Walt Disney Presents"** is television's first stereophonic broadcast.

Americans see first newsreel film for television transmitted across the ocean by telephone cable—footage of Queen Mother and Princess Margaret waving goodbye to Queen Elizabeth as she leaves for Canada.

Yea, but can he sing country

Clean cut crooner Columbia grad Pat Boone invests in two radio stations – one in Nashville and one in Fort Worth.

But Your Honor, Going Back To Dating Is Hell

In the first nationally televised murder trial, 45-year old divorcee, Mrs. Connie Nicholas, is tried and found guilty of manslaughter for the murder of her lover of 15 years, Forrest Teel, 54, executive vice-president of Eli Lilly & Co., who left her for a younger woman.

The Federal Communications Commission opens hearings on television crime.

The "Equal Time" law is amended allowing coverage of political news and candidates without being obligated to give an equal amount of free time to other competing candidates.

P A S S I N G S

Beloved to several generations of youngsters, **Carl Switzer**, goofy Alfalfa on "Our Gang," dies after a fight turns deadly at the age of 31.

George Reeves, who as television's super hero Superman could ward off any foe of disaster, shoots himself at age 45, several days before his intended marriage.

Lou Costello, who along with partner Bud Abbott, comprised one of the best-loved comedy teams in the history of show business, dies several days before his 51st birthday. Among their many successes in theatre, radio, movies and television, their "Who's on First" skit remains one of the classic comic routines of all time.

WHAT A YEAR IT WAS!

1959 POPULAR SONGS

MUSIC

16 Candles.............................	*Crests*
77 Sunset Strip	*TV Theme Song*
A Big Hunk O' Love	*Elvis Presley*
A Fool Such As I......................	*Elvis Presley*
A Teenager In Love..................	*Dion & The Belmonts*
Alvin's Harmonica...................	*Chipmunks*
Among My Souvenirs...............	*Connie Francis*
Battle Hymn of the Republic ...	*Mormon Tabernacle Choir*
The Battle of New Orleans......	*Johnny Horton*
Be My Guest............................	*Fats Domino*
Broken-Hearted Melody	*Sarah Vaughan*
Charlie Brown.........................	*Coasters*
Climb Ev'ry Mountain.............	*The Sound of Music*
Come Softly To Me	*Fleetwoods*
Danny Boy	*Conway Twitty*
Donna......................................	*Ritchie Valens*
Do-Re-Mi	*The Sound of Music*
Dream Lover	*Bobby Darin*
Enchanted................................	*Platters*
Everything's Coming Up Roses	*Ethel Merman*
Goodbye Jimmy, Goodbye.......	*Ruby Murray*
The Happy Organ....................	*Dave "Baby" Cortez*
Heartaches By The Number	*Guy Mitchell*
High Hopes	*Frank Sinatra*
Hound Dog Man.......................	*Fabian*
I Know....................................	*Perry Como*
I Only Have Eyes For You	*Flamingos*
I've Waited So Long................	*Anthony Newley*
Jingle Bell Rock	*Max Bygraves*
Just A Little Too Much............	*Ricky Nelson*
Kansas City.............................	*Wilbur Harrison*
Kookie, Kookie (Lend Me Your Comb)	*Edd Byrnes & Connie Stevens*
Lipstick On Your Collar...........	*Connie Francis*
Lonely Boy..............................	*Paul Anka*
Mack The Knife	*Bobby Darin*
Mr. Blue	*Fleetwoods*
My Happiness...........................	*Connie Francis*
Never Be Anyone Else But You	*Ricky Nelson*
Only Sixteen	*Craig Douglas*
Peggy Sue Got Married...........	*Buddy Holly*
Personality	*Lloyd Price*
Peter Gunn Theme...................	*Duane Eddy*
Pillow Talk	*Doris Day*
Poison Ivy	*Coasters*
Put Your Head On My Shoulder.....................	*Paul Anka*
Ragtime Cowboy Joe...............	*Chipmunks*
Sea of Love	*Phil Phillips with the Twilights*
Since I Don't Have You	*Skyliners*
Sixteen Going On Seventeen....	*The Sound of Music*
Sleep Walk	*Santo & Johnny*
Smoke Gets In Your Eyes........	*Platters*
Someone..................................	*Johnny Mathis*
The Sound Of Music................	*Mary Martin*
Stagger Lee.............................	*Lloyd Price*
Sweeter Than You	*Ricky Nelson*
Take A Message To Mary	*Everly Brothers*
There Goes My Baby...............	*Drifters*
The Three Bells	*Browns*
Tijuana Jail.............................	*Kingston Trio*
('Til) I Kissed You..................	*Everly Brothers*
Venus......................................	*Frankie Avalon*
Way Down Yonder in New Orleans	*Freddy Cannon*
What A Difference A Day Makes	*Dinah Washington*
What'd I Say (Pt. 1)................	*Ray Charles*
Why	*Frankie Avalon*

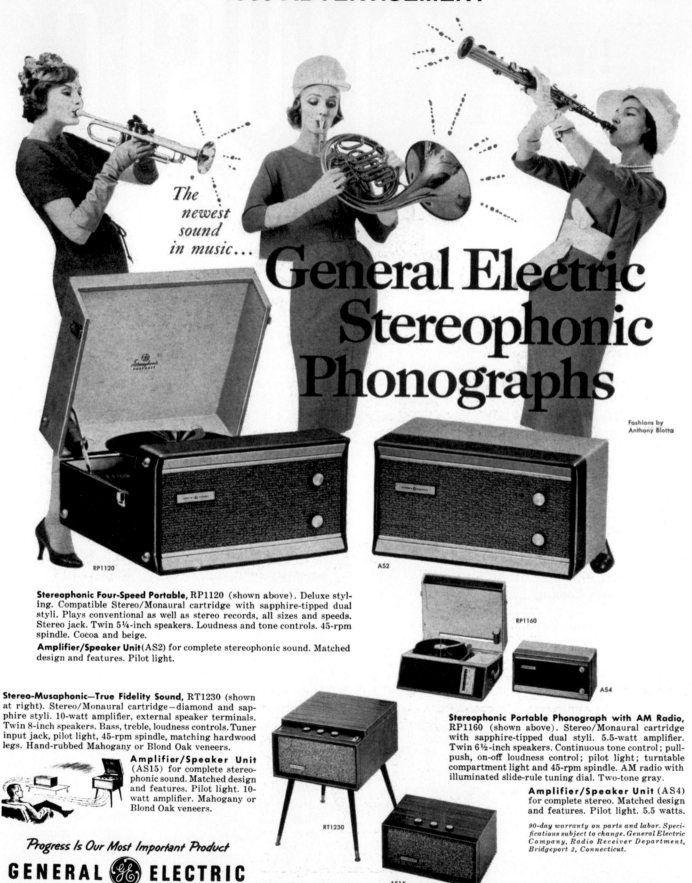

The newest sound in music...

General Electric Stereophonic Phonographs

Fashions by
Anthony Blotta

RP1120

AS2

RP1160

AS4

Stereophonic Four-Speed Portable, RP1120 (shown above). Deluxe styling. Compatible Stereo/Monaural cartridge with sapphire-tipped dual styli. Plays conventional as well as stereo records, all sizes and speeds. Stereo jack. Twin 5¼-inch speakers. Loudness and tone controls. 45-rpm spindle. Cocoa and beige.

Amplifier/Speaker Unit (AS2) for complete stereophonic sound. Matched design and features. Pilot light.

Stereo-Musaphonic—True Fidelity Sound, RT1230 (shown at right). Stereo/Monaural cartridge—diamond and sapphire styli. 10-watt amplifier, external speaker terminals. Twin 8-inch speakers. Bass, treble, loudness controls. Tuner input jack, pilot light, 45-rpm spindle, matching hardwood legs. Hand-rubbed Mahogany or Blond Oak veneers.

Amplifier/Speaker Unit (AS15) for complete stereophonic sound. Matched design and features. Pilot light. 10-watt amplifier. Mahogany or Blond Oak veneers.

Stereophonic Portable Phonograph with AM Radio, RP1160 (shown above). Stereo/Monaural cartridge with sapphire-tipped dual styli. 5.5-watt amplifier. Twin 6½-inch speakers. Continuous tone control; pull-push, on-off loudness control; pilot light; turntable compartment light and 45-rpm spindle. AM radio with illuminated slide-rule tuning dial. Two-tone gray.

Amplifier/Speaker Unit (AS4) for complete stereo. Matched design and features. Pilot light. 5.5 watts.

90-day warranty on parts and labor. Specifications subject to change. General Electric Company, Radio Receiver Department, Bridgeport 2, Connecticut.

RT1230

AS15

Progress Is Our Most Important Product

GENERAL ⒼⒺ **ELECTRIC**

New Pop Recording Stars

**ANNETTE FUNICELLO
BROOK BENTON
CHUBBY CHECKER
JAMES DARREN
FABIAN
ISLEY BROTHERS
JAN & DEAN*
CLIFF RICHARD
BOBBY RYDELL
BOBBY VEE**

* Picked #1 New Group By Record Fans

BRITAIN GETS ITS FIRST
TEEN IDOL—
Cliff Richard

Headliners at the
SANDS HOTEL, LAS VEGAS
● ● ● ● ● ● ● ● ●

Frank Sinatra	Dean Martin
Tony Bennett	Joey Bishop
Nat "King" Cole	Johnny Mathis
Sammy Davis, Jr.	Danny Thomas
Lena Horne	Louis Armstrong
Rowan & Martin	Bobby Darin

With the biggest selling pop record in the U. S., **BOBBY DARIN'S** "Mack The Knife" catapults him into a headliner for the first time at the Sands Hotel in Las Vegas with his gross income for 1959 estimated at $250,000.

Folk rockers the KINGSTON TRIO sell more records than Fabian.

"Puppy Love" is first single recorded by 13-year old DOLLY PARTON.

Her performance at the Newport Folk Festival wins recognition for JOAN BAEZ.

Bing's Boys

Estranged from their famous father, **Gary, Philip, Lindsay** and **Dennis Crosby** open their act at the Sahara Hotel in Las Vegas sans **Der Bingel** who is off on an Alaskan fishing trip.

WHAT A YEAR IT WAS!

1959

Count Basie

Sonny Rollins

SONNY ROLLINS practices his tenor sax every day on New York's Williamsburg Bridge after he stops performing.

MILES DAVIS' "Buzzard Song" is a major hit.

ALL THAT JAZZ AND MORE

New York's Randall's Island is site of the world's biggest jam session featuring the great Dave Brubeck and his classical and traditional jazz fusion quartet dominating the event with "West Coast Jazz" trumpeter Miles Davis receiving accolades for his Miles Davis Sextet.

Paris resident American jazz singer **Josephine Baker** comes out of retirement to star in new review **Paris Mes Amours** at the Olympia Music Hall.

Alan Lomax returns to the south to further research traditional American music and culture.

The King Of Swing Is Swinging Again

After several slow years, the inimitable **Benny Goodman** is flying high again as he completes a triumphant European tour and opens his first nightclub appearance in two years at New York's famed Basin Street East.

Benny Goodman

WHAT A YEAR IT WAS!

FAMOUS BIRTHS

Bryan Adams
Sheena Easton
Kathy Mattea
Marie Osmond
Richie Sambora
Randy Travis

Passings

"Lady Day," beloved singer **Billie Holiday**, whose talent for singing jazz and blues was incomparable, dies at the age of 44. For her many fans throughout the world, she leaves behind such memorable recordings as "STRANGE FRUIT," "FINE AND MELLOW" and "LOVER MAN."

On tour in the mid-west with the Winter Dance Party, young rock 'n' roll stars **Buddy Holly**, **Ritchie Valens** and the "Big Bopper" **J.P. Richardson** were on their way from Iowa to North Dakota when their chartered plane crashed, killing everyone on board. All three had enjoyed hit songs, including Holly's "THAT'LL BE THE DAY," Valens' "LA BAMBA" and Richardson's "CHANTILLY LACE."

Saxophonist **Sidney Bechet**, legendary Storyville jazz musician who was even more famous abroad than the U.S., dies in France at age 62.

Tenor sax player **Lester Young**, onetime member of Count Basie's band who also played with Billie Holiday and Benny Goodman, dies at age 50.

Writer of the classic song "FOR ME AND MY GAL," **George W. Meyer**, 75, dies in a Manhattan hotel fire.

"CHATTANOOGA CHOO-CHOO" lyricist **Mack Gordon** dies of a heart attack at age 54.

Creator of timeless songs "TAKE ME OUT TO THE BALL GAME" and "SHINE ON, HARVEST MOON," lyricist **Jack Norworth**, dies at age 80.

Put Away Them Blue Suede Shoes And Take Out Those White Bucks

The faces of rock 'n' roll are changing. **Elvis Presley** is still in the Army, **Buddy Holly** and **Ritchie Valens** are dead, **Jerry Lee Lewis** is *persona non grata* because of his marriage to his underage cousin and **Chuck Berry** is also in trouble for bringing a minor across state lines. With these icons gone new, clean-cut faces begin to take over the pop music scene and we hear the music of **Pat Boone**, **James Darren**, **Frankie Avalon**, **Bobby Rydell**, **Fabian** and **Edd "Kookie" Byrnes** hit the radio airwaves.

♪ **Dick Clark's national tour of "Caravan of Stars," fueled by the success of his American Bandstand television show on ABC, brings in audiences in record numbers across the country.**

♪ **On the heels of a House sub-committee investigating payola in the music business, ABC forces Dick Clark to give up his interest in Swan Records when it is discovered that the rock 'n' roll recording of "Way Down Yonder" being plugged on American Bandstand was issued by... you guessed it... Swan Records.**

♪ **Rock 'n' roll idol Alan Freed's contract is terminated by WABC when he refuses to sign an affidavit that he took bribes from record companies.**

Grammy
Awards

Song Of The Year
The Battle Of New Orleans
Jimmy Driftwood, songwriter

Record Of The Year
Mack The Knife
Bobby Darin

Best New Artist
Bobby Darin

Best Male Vocal Performance
Come Dance With Me
Frank Sinatra

Best Female Vocal Performance
But Not For Me
Ella Fitzgerald

**Best Performance
By A Top 40 Artist**
Midnight Flyer
Nat "King" Cole

Comedy Performance
Inside Shelley Berman
Shelley Berman

Spoken Word
A Lincoln Portrait
Carl Sandburg

RINGO GETS HIS FIRST BIG BANG

Ringo Starr joins
RORY STORM AND THE HURRICANES.

Neil Sedaka gives up his classical concert studies, switches to the world of rock 'n' roll and co-creates with Howard Greenfield "Oh! Carol" which hits the top ten.

MINE EYES HAVE SEEN THE TOP TEN ON THE CHARTS

"The Battle Hymn Of The Republic" recording by the Mormon Tabernacle Choir, backed by the Philadelphia Symphony Orchestra, stuns the pop world by becoming a hit!

Having more than a few nips of the sauce before his recording session of "White Lightning," **George Jones** does 83 takes before it's a wrap.

DIRTY IS IN THE EAR OF THE LISTENER

Randy Wood, President of Dot Records, stops distribution of collaborative effort by Beat poet Jack Kerouac and jazz pianist Steve Allen calling the material on "Poetry Of The Beat Generation" in poor taste and not suitable for children.

Recovering after being beset with personal and professional problems, **Judy Garland's** husband, Sid Luft, books her into the Metropolitan Opera House for her official come-back where devoted fans will hear "Somewhere Over The Rainbow" and "The Trolley Song."

BREAKING INTO REAL ROCK

Actor/singer Pat Boone breaks his toe on a Hollywood set when he kicks what he thinks is a paper mache rock that turns out to be a stone.

ON BROADWAY

With Advance Sales In Excess Of Two Million Dollars, Rodgers & Hammerstein's THE SOUND OF MUSIC Opens To Rave Reviews And Is Called An Inescapable Crowd Pleaser.

Mary Martin on the left, with Kathy Dunn, Evanna Lien, Mary Susan Locke, Lauri Peters, Marilyn Rogers, William Snowden and Joseph Stewart.

ANOTHER OPENING, ANOTHER NIGHT

Melvyn
Douglas

**THE GANG'S
ALL HERE**

**A TOUCH OF
THE POET**

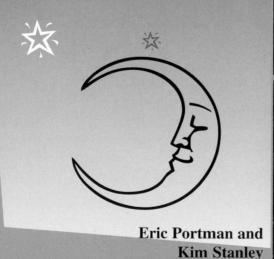

Eric Portman and
Kim Stanley

From left, Robert Coote, Rex Harrison and Julie Andrews

"MY FAIR LADY" BECOMES MY RICH LADY

"My Fair Lady" Celebrates Its Third Anniversary Surpassing $10,000,000 In Sales, Smashing Box Office Records On Four Continents.

SOMETHING TO BEAT THE DRUMS ABOUT

Off-Broadway Musical Production Of "The Threepenny Opera" Celebrates Its History-Making Run With 1,405 Performances.

TO PAY OR NOT TO PAY... THAT IS THE QUESTION

Joseph Papp Wins Battle With New York City Park Commissioner Robert Moses And Presents Free Shakespeare In The Park.

ON BROADWAY

A Loss Of Roses

A Majority Of One

A Raisin In The Sun

A Touch Of The Poet

Destry Rides Again

The Devil's Disciple

The Disenchanted

Fiorello!

Flower Drum Song

The Gang's All Here

The Girls Against The Boys

Goodbye Charlie

The Great God Brown

Gypsy

WHAT A YEAR IT WAS!

137

1959

The Stars At Night Are Bigger And Brighter

A London High School Is Dazzled By Cowboy Version Of "A Midsummer Night's Dream" Presented By An Acting Troupe From Howard Payne College Of Brownswood, Texas.

•

Second City Improvisational Troupe Begin Their Antics In Chicago.

•

After A Record 26-Year Run At The Theatre Mart In Los Angeles, "The Drunkard" Finally Closes.

•

Sir Laurence Olivier, Recognized As The Greatest Living Actor, Even Dazzled The Critics With His Brilliant Performance In Shakespeare's "Coriolanus" At The Stratford-On-Avon Production.

•

There's No Such Thing As A Small Part, Only A Small... Oh Well You Know The Rest

Academy Award Winner Shirley Booth Leaves Pulitzer Prize Winner William Inge's New Play "A Loss Of Roses" (Co-Starring Carol Haney And Warren Beatty) Before Its Broadway Opening On The Grounds That Her Part Is Not Important Enough.

Passings

Playwright **Maxwell Anderson**, whose work includes "What Price Glory" and "Bad Seed," as well as the Pulitzer Prize winning "Both Your Houses," dies at age 70.

Grand Dame of the theatre and member of the famed Drew-Barrymore thespians, **Ethel Barrymore**, who starred in only one film with her brothers John and Lionel, "Rasputin And The Empress," dies at age 79. Her supposed last words are "Is everybody happy... I know I'm happy."

Kay Kendall, actress in both theatre and film and wife of Rex Harrison, dies at age 33 of leukemia.

Mark Twain Tonight!

The Marriage-Go-Round

The Miracle Worker

Moonbirds

Much Ado About Nothing

My Fair Lady

Once Upon A Mattress

Only In America

Our Town

The Pleasure Of His Company

Rashomon

Requiem For A Nun

The Sound Of Music

Sweet Bird Of Youth

West Side Story

Tony Awards
1959

OUTSTANDING PLAY
"J. B."
Archibald MacLeish

OUTSTANDING MUSICAL
"REDHEAD"

OUTSTANDING DRAMATIC ACTOR
JASON ROBARDS, JR.
"The Disenchanted"

OUTSTANDING DRAMATIC ACTRESS
GERTRUDE BERG
"A Majority Of One"

OUTSTANDING MUSICAL ACTOR
RICHARD KILEY
"Redhead"

OUTSTANDING MUSICAL ACTRESS
GWEN VERDON
"Redhead"

OUTSTANDING DIRECTOR
ELIA KAZAN
"J. B."

OUTSTANDING CHOREOGRAPHER
BOB FOSSE
"Redhead"

SPECIAL AWARDS

JOHN GIELGUD
For contributions to the theatre and for his extraordinary insight into the writings of Shakespeare as demonstrated in his one-man play "Ages of Man."

HOWARD LINDSAY and **RUSSELL CROUSE**
For a collaboration that has lasted longer than Gilbert and Sullivan.

Drama Critics' Circle bypass Tennessee Williams' "Sweet Bird Of Youth" and Archibald MacLeish's "J. B." naming Lorraine Hansberry's "A Raisin In The Sun" Best American Play making her the first Negro writer to earn this coveted award.

Hollywood's First Academy Award Winner, Silent Film Star Janet Gaynor, Comes Out Of A 20-Year Retirement To Make Her Stage Debut In Joseph Hayes' New Play, "The Midnight Sun."

•

ROUNDING OUT THE PERFORMANCE

New York's Wollman Skating Rink is the site of new theatre-in-the-round designed by esteemed architect Edward D. Stone.

•

The Living Theatre's Off-Broadway Avant-Garde Production Of Jack Gelber's "The Connection" Shocks Critics With Its Controversial Drug Theme And Breaking Of The Fourth Wall.

•

France's Highest Paid And Most Popular Entertainer, Singer Yves Montand, Wows Critics In American Debut At Manhattan's Henry Miller Theatre.

•

Star Of "J. B.," Pat Hingle, Seriously Injured In 30-Foot Plunge Down Elevator Shaft.

•

Opening Its 100th Season, American Actor Paul Robeson Stars In The Stratford-On-Avon Production Of "Otello" Following His Eight-Year Travel Ban By The U. S. Government.

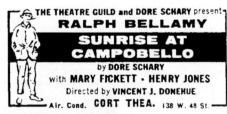

Dance

- The New York City Ballet Does U. S. Premiere Of KURT WEILL'S "The Seven Deadly Sins."

- NOEL COWARD'S First Ballet, "London Morning" Falls On Its... Toes.

- JEROME ROBBINS' Ballets U.S.A. Receives Wide Acclaim During Its European Tour.

- DANCE HISTORY IS MADE When Martha Graham Joins Forces with George Balanchine And The New York City Ballet In A Production Called "Episodes."

Thanks to the remarkable efforts of impresario **SOL HUROK**, Moscow's Bolshoi Ballet arrives in New York for a 2-month tour of America and Canada and spends their first night at the circus at Madison Square Garden eating one of America's food favorites—the good old hot dog.

The Bolshoi's prima ballerina, 49-year old **GALINA ULANOVA** dazzled the who's who of communism with her work in *Giselle* at a 16-curtain call performance commemorating the 21st World Congress Of The Communist Party. The incomparable dancer appears on opening night at the Metropolitan Opera House in *Romeo and Juliet* winning highest critical acclaim for her work.

Royal Ballet prima ballerina **Margot Fonteyn** is detained by the Panamanian government on the suspicion of being involved in a plot to overthrow the government. Her husband, Roberto Arias, escapes being captured by jumping onto a passing shrimp boat.

In an effort to develop its own dancers, the Metropolitan Opera presents a performance of its resident ballet company for the first time.

Britain's oldest dance company, the Ballet Rambert, makes its American debut at Jacob's Pillow, Massachusetts.

Patricia Wilde and Jacques d'Amboise dance in Balanchine's "Native Dancers" inspired by a famous race horse.

Gagaku, the dancers of the Japanese Imperial household, make their American debut under the auspices of the New York City Ballet.

NEW YORK CITY'S LICENSE COMMISSIONER ORDERS THE FEMALE DANCERS OF LES BALLETS AFRICAINS TO COVER UP WHEN HE DISCOVERS THEY ARE NAKED FROM THE WAIST UP.

WHAT A YEAR IT WAS!

1959

Classical Music

Leonard Bernstein and the New York Philharmonic receive unprecedented accolades by the tough Russian audiences after his reading of Shostakovich's "Fifth Symphony" calling it the best interpretation ever heard.

Under the auspices of the State Department **Leonard Bernstein** and the New York Philharmonic begin a 50-concert international tour covering 29 cities in 17 countries.

TURKISH DELIGHT

Music-hungry Turks crash through wooden police barricades at Istanbul's open-air theatre packing aisles and stairs to hear **Leonard Bernstein** conduct the 106-piece New York Philharmonic Orchestra.

Under the direction of **Leonard Bernstein**, the New York Philharmonic and the Dave Brubeck Quartet join together for *"Dialogues for Jazz Combo and Orchestra."*

As part of the cultural exchange program six Soviet musicians including Dmitri Shostakovich visit the U. S.

SHOSTAKOVICH

Dmitri Shostakovich breaks ranks with symphonic tradition and puts a Lindy Hop into his first opera called "Moskva, Cheromushki."

And then they wrote...

Second String Quartet
Elliott Carter

Symphony No. 7
David Diamond

A Hand of Bridge
Gian-Carlo Menotti & Samuel Barber

Concerto for Piano and Orchestra
Walter Piston

Variations for Violin and Orchestra
Wallingford Riegger

Three Moods
William Schuman

Conversations (concertino)
Gunther Schuller

Collected Poems
Virgil Thomson

WHAT A YEAR IT WAS!

1959

OPERA NEWS

PASSING OUT THOSE GREEN NOTES

The Rockefeller Foundation makes a joint grant of $175,000 to Columbia and Princeton universities to be used to expand research and development in the field of electronic sounds.

PABLO CASALS

opens the third Casals Music Festival in San Juan, Puerto Rico.

Pulitzer Prize For Music

Concerto For Piano And Orchestra

John La Montaine

Anyone Ever Hear Of Equal Pay?

Mezzo diva Rise Stevens cancels her 13-week contract at the San Francisco Opera Company after she learns Italian tenor Mario del Monaco is being paid more per performance.

•

A Colorado centennial production of Puccini's "The Girl Of The Golden West" is staged western style at Colorado's Red Rocks Theatre.

•

Metropolitan Opera House's production of Alban Berg's controversial atonal "Wozzeck" receives twenty-minute opening night ovation.

•

Swedish diva Birgit Nilsson makes victorious debut in Metropolitan Opera's production of "Tristan und Isolde."

•

A musical play based on Pirandello's "Six Characters in Search of an Author" is produced by the New York City Opera.

Recovering from an automobile accident which put her in traction, coloratura soprano **Dolores Wilson** removes her neck brace and fills in for ailing **Lily Pons** who was to sing in "Lucia di Lammermoor" at the Met. Unfortunately, Miss Wilson finds herself back in the hospital in traction after suffering a collapse following her performance.

MARIA CALLAS and VAN CLIBURN pack the house at the Philadelphia Academy of Music where tickets are selling at up to $100 a pop.

Tempestuous diva MARIA CALLAS is furious when she learns young Australian soprano JOAN SUTHERLAND is hired by La Scala.

Passings

38-year old opera singer **Mario Lanza** dies of a heart attack. The singer turned actor starred in "THE GREAT CARUSO" and will be remembered for his hit songs "LOVELIEST NIGHT OF THE YEAR" and "BE MY LOVE" each of which sold well over a million copies.

Composer **Heitor Villa-Lobos**, the most famous and respected Brazilian music man of his era, dies at age 75.

WHAT A YEAR IT WAS!

Zenith puts all its quality, its famous features, into new, slim portable-table TV

All-new—trim, Slim Classic design. Sets the style pace in portable TV. And only Zenith Portable TV has the handcrafted horizontal chassis to give you world-famous Zenith big-set performance. Sound-out-front speaker. The Zenith LaSalle, Model D1811C† in charcoal, $199.95.*

New slim, trim styling in a table model—blends with the decor of any room. Extra picture contrast from Zenith's Sunshine picture tube and Cinelens. Spotlight dial. The Zenith Gotham, Model D2317** in grained mahogany, walnut or blonde oak colors, $239.95*.

First time ever! Space Command® remote TV control in Zenith portable TV. Relax, don't get up. Tune TV from across the room with silent sound—no wires, no cords, no batteries.

Just touch a button on the control unit you hold in your hand—to change channels, turn set on and off, adjust volume, mute sound.

And only Zenith has it!

THE NEW LOOK IN TV IS THE SLIM CLASSIC LOOK! New, slim, trim Zenith portable-table TV fits beautifully, even in bookshelf space, in your living room, den, or bedroom.

See the world's most talked-about television at your Zenith dealer's!

ZENITH RADIO CORPORATION, CHICAGO 39, ILLINOIS. The Royalty of television, stereophonic high fidelity instruments, phonographs, radios and hearing aids, 41 years of leadership in radionics exclusively. *Manufacturer's suggested retail price. Slightly higher in the Southwest and West Coast. Prices and specifications subject to change without notice.

ZENITH ®

The quality goes in before the name goes on

144

ON VIEW AT THE CHICAGO ART INSTITUTE are three recently found Paul Gauguin drawings.

THE ROBERT LEHMAN COLLECTION, largest private art collection in America, is on view at the Cincinnati Museum.

TO SAVE MONEY, THE MUSEUM OF MODERN ART closes its doors on Mondays.

THE $400,000 Gertrude Vanderbilt Whitney Gallery of Western Art opens in Cody, Wyoming.

THE MUSEUM OF MODERN ART in Manhattan begins efforts to raise $25 million for a new addition to the overcrowded museum.

VICTIM OF THE LARGEST ART HEIST IN CANADIAN HISTORY, the Toronto Art Gallery loses six paintings worth more than $600,000 by Rembrandt, Renoir and Rubens. The canvases are found several weeks later in a garage.

AVERY BRUNDAGE AGREES TO DONATE his Oriental art collection to San Francisco and the city will expand its M.H. De Young Memorial Museum to accommodate the massive contribution.

RETROSPECTIVES AND SHOWS

PIERRE BONNARD at Phillips Gallery, Washington, DC
MARC CHAGALL at Musee des Arts Decoratifs du Louvre, Paris
SIR WINSTON CHURCHILL at Royal Academy of Arts, London
ROBERT DE NIRO at Ellison Gallery, Fort Worth, Texas
PAUL GAUGUIN at Art Institute of Chicago
WINSLOW HOMER at Museum of Fine Arts, Boston
JASPER JOHNS at Galerie Rive Droite, Paris
RENE MAGRITTE at Bodley, New York
JOAN MIRO at Museum of Modern Art, New York
CLAUDE MONET at Galerie Durand-Ruel, Paris
MAN RAY at Institute of Contemporary Arts, London
MAX WEBER at Newark Museum, New Jersey

Prince Rainier hires Italian artist Renato Signorini to sculpt an 18 carat gold bust of Princess Grace.

Gina Lollobrigida, Celeste Holm, Jose Ferrer and **Barbara Bel Geddes** are some of the celebrity artists included in the United Nations Art Club exhibition; proceeds benefit UNICEF.

From Histoire Naturelle

MAX ERNST at Musee d'Art Moderne, Paris

1959 CREATIONS

Louise Nevelson
"Dawn's Wedding Feast"

Isamu Noguchi
"Integral"

Jasper Johns
"Numbers In Color"

Yves Klein
"IKB 79"

Robert Rauschenberg
"Canyon"

Ad Reinhardt
"Abstract Painting, 1959"

Marcel Duchamp
"With My Tongue In My Cheek"

AUCTIONS
Sotheby & Company, London

Peter Paul Rubens (record high price for a painting)
Adoration of the Magi $ 770,000

El Greco
The Apostle James the Greater   201,600

Pablo Picasso (record high for a painting by a living artist)
La Belle Hollandaise   154,000

Paul Cezanne
Portrait of his wife   112,000

Georges Braque
Femme a la Mandoline   100,800

Thomas Gainsborough
Countess of Chesterfield   95,200

Parke-Bernet Galleries, New York

Pierre August Renoir
Les Filles de Durand-Ruel   255,000

Henri de Toulouse-Lautrec
Femme Rousse dans un Jardin   180,000

PABLO PICASSO'S six bronze sculptures, **"Bathers,"** are for sale at Manhattan's Fine Art Associates Gallery for $250,000

JASPER JOHNS' TARGET IS ACQUIRED BY THE MUSEUM OF MODERN ART, NY

Marie Antoinette's diamond necklace, along with baubles belonging to Queen Elizabeth and jeweler Harry Winston, help comprise "The Ageless Diamond" exhibition at Christie's in London. At Sotheby's, Winston purchases the "Westminster Tiara," 1,240 diamonds for $308,000.

WHO TOOK DA TUT?
In Cairo, museum officials announce the disappearance of King Tutankhamen's scepter.

Workmen in Athens uncover an ancient bronze of the god Apollo, and archaeologists attribute the work to the 6th century sculptor Antenor.

Salvador Dali
informs POPE JOHN XXIII of his desire to create a new church in Texas.

MARC CHAGALL is elected an Honorary Member of the American Academy of Arts and Letters. He is also named first artist-in-residence at Brandeis University in Massachusetts.

Starry, Starry Night
Planetariums open at the Boston Museum of Science and the Cleveland Natural History Museum.

Controversy rages in Los Angeles as the Building and Safety Department insists on conducting severe tests on the WATTS TOWERS to determine if the structures are sturdy enough to remain standing.

But It Speaks To Me
Swedish artist **Oyvind Fahlstrom** furiously removes one of his paintings from a Stockholm exhibit. Yes, the piece in question is his, but no, it isn't a painting. It is only packing to secure the pieces that he sent for the show.

Thousands watch as a 91-foot statue of Jesus Christ is dedicated in Portugal.

WHAT A YEAR IT WAS!

At the Carnegie International Exhibition in Pittsburgh, sculptor *Alexander Calder* wins first prize in sculpture.

The United States Exhibition in Moscow is seen by over 2 1/2 million Russians. Some artists represented include *Jackson Pollock*, *Robert Motherwell*, *Willem de Kooning*, *Mark Rothko* and *Andrew Wyeth*.

The first Paris Biennale exhibits over five hundred artists under 35 from forty-two countries.

Blind artists are the focus of a New York show, and their paintings, ceramics and sculpture are of such a high standard that it's impossible to tell they were created by people without sight.

Art owned by IBM, CBS, DeBeers and other businesses is on view at the "Art: USA: 59" presentation in New York.

PASSINGS

Dada Artist GEORGE GROSZ, whose satirical portraits of German life invoked the ire of the Nazis, emigrated to the United States to avoid persecution. He returned to his hometown of Berlin only weeks before his death of a heart attack at age 65.

The Absolute Monarchist by Grosz

1959 ADVERTISEMENT

A NEW KIND OF PORTABLE FROM ROYAL

The FUTURA* is the first and only portable with ALL the practical features of a standard office typewriter:

❶ Famous Magic® Margin... ❷ exclusive Twin-Pak®, the easy-change ribbon... ❸ new Magic® Column Set key for automatic keyboard tabulation... ❹ Royal Touch Control®... ❺ handy Line Meter, page-end indicator... ❻ Royal's *full* standard keyboard...

❼ finger-flow keys... ❽ comfortable keyboard slope... plus ❾ one-piece, unitized construction for rugged, rugged wear. All yours in your choice of four gay colors and handsome, luggage-type case. Ask your Royal Portable dealer about his Easy-Payment Plan.

See the new ROYALITE Portable—easy to carry—easy to use—yet so rugged! Full-sized keyboard. And the price is surprisingly *low!*

 World's most wanted portable

*Trademark of Royal McBee Corp.   World's Largest Manufacturer of Typewriters.

books

E.E. Cummings
100 POEMS

Allen Drury
ADVISE AND CONSENT

Margaret Mead
AN ANTHROPOLOGIST AT WORK

Mordecai Richler
THE APPRENTICESHIP OF DUDDY KRAVITZ

Moss Hart
ACT ONE

Italo Calvino
THE BARON IN THE TREES

Robert St. John
BEN-GURION: THE BIOGRAPHY OF AN EXTRAORDINARY MAN

Brendan Behan
THE BORSTAL BOY

Truman Capote
BREAKFAST AT TIFFANY'S

Frederic Sondern, Jr.
BROTHERHOOD OF EVIL: THE MAFIA

Joyce Cary
THE CAPTIVE AND THE FREE

Robert Penn Warren
THE CAVE

Aldous Huxley
COLLECTED ESSAYS

Pearl S. Buck
COMMAND THE MORNING

Sir Vivian Fuchs & Sir Edmund Hillary
THE CROSSING OF ANTARCTICA

Salvador Dali
DALI ON MODERN ART

Taylor Caldwell
DEAR AND GLORIOUS PHYSICIAN

Jack Kerouac
DOCTOR SAX

Milton Berle & John Roeburt
EARTHQUAKE

William Strunk, Jr. & E.B. White
THE ELEMENTS OF STYLE

Richard Carrington
ELEPHANTS

Elspeth Huxley
THE FLAME TREES OF THIKA

C.G. Jung
FLYING SAUCERS: A MODERN MYTH OF THINGS SEEN IN THE SKIES

Dr. DeForest Clinton Jarvis
FOLK MEDICINE

John O'Hara
FROM THE TERRACE

Harry Golden
FOR 2¢ PLAIN

Ian Fleming
GOLDFINGER

Philip Roth
GOODBYE, COLUMBUS AND FIVE SHORT STORIES

Mae West
GOODNESS HAD NOTHING TO DO WITH IT

Shirley Jackson
THE HAUNTING OF HILL HOUSE

James A. Michener
HAWAII

Saul Bellow
HENDERSON THE RAIN KING

Vladimir Nabokov
INVITATION TO A BEHEADING

Sacheverell Sitwell
JOURNEY TO THE ENDS OF TIME

Leonard Bernstein
THE JOY OF MUSIC

Romain Gary
LADY L

Boris Pasternak
THE LAST SUMMER

Evelyn Wood Reading Dynamics Institute opens in Washington.

Allen Ginsberg and **Gregory Corso** are two of the participants in a reading of Beat poets at Columbia University.

Mystery writer **Raymond Chandler,** whose Philip Marlowe character remains the most popular detective in literature, dies at age 70. His books include "The Big Sleep," "Farewell, My Lovely" and "The Lady In The Lake."

Creator of the notorious Fu Manchu character, writer **Sax Rohmer** dies in London at or around age 75.

Duncan Hines, author of books that guide travelers to good places to stay and eat, dies at age 78.

Federal Judge Frederick Van Pelt Bryan rules the U. S. Post Office ban on the unexpurgated American edition of D.H. Lawrence's "Lady Chatterley's Lover" is unconstitutional.

In Alabama, "The Rabbits' Wedding," a children's book about two married rabbits, is forced into the back rooms of libraries, available only by specific inquiry. The brouhaha is brought about because some lawmakers are convinced the married rabbits—one black, one white—are urging mixed marriages.

WHAT A YEAR IT WAS!

Aldous Huxley is the recipient of the American Academy of Arts and Letters Award of Merit medal. **Arthur Miller** receives the Gold Medal for drama.

Charles van Doren, ed.
LETTERS TO MOTHER: AN ANTHOLOGY

Grace Paley
THE LITTLE DISTURBANCES OF MAN

Ira Gershwin
LYRICS ON SEVERAL OCCASIONS

Jack Kerouac
MAGGIE CASSIDY

Richard Condon
THE MANCHURIAN CANDIDATE

William Faulkner
THE MANSION

Simone de Beauvoir
MEMOIRS OF A DUTIFUL DAUGHTER

Laurie Lee
MOMENT OF WAR

Ira Wallace
MUSCLE BEACH

Jack Douglas
MY BROTHER WAS AN ONLY CHILD

Bertrand Russell
MY PHILOSOPHICAL DEVELOPMENT

Mary Astor
MY STORY: AN AUTOBIOGRAPHY

V.S. Naipaul
THE MYSTIC MASSEUR

William Burroughs
NAKED LUNCH

OBSERVATIONS
Photographs by Richard Avedon, Commentary by Truman Capote

Pablo Picasso
PICASSO DRAWINGS: FROM 1900 TO THE PRESENT

W. Somerset Maugham
POINTS OF VIEW

George D. Painter
PROUST: THE EARLY YEARS

Vladimir Nabokov
THE REAL LIFE OF SEBASTIAN KNIGHT

Grace Metalious
RETURN TO PEYTON PLACE

John Updike
THE SAME DOOR

Kurt Vonnegut
THE SIRENS OF TITAN

Arthur Koestler
THE SLEEPWALKERS

Robert A. Heinlein
STARSHIP TROOPERS

Colin Wilson
THE STATURE OF MAN

Vance Packard
THE STATUS SEEKERS

Fred Astaire
STEPS IN TIME

Peter De Vries
THE TENTS OF WICKEDNESS

Israel Cohen
THEODORE HERZL: FOUNDER OF POLITICAL ZIONISM

Herman Wouk
THIS IS MY GOD

Thomas Griffith
WAIST-HIGH CULTURE

Samuel Beckett
WATT

Bertrand Russell
WISDOM OF THE WEST

James Thurber
THE YEARS WITH ROSS

PRIZES

NOBEL

Literature:

SALVATORE QUASIMODO, ITALY

PULITZER

Fiction:

ROBERT LEWIS TAYLOR
THE TRAVELS OF JAIMIE MCPHEETERS

Poetry:

STANLEY KUNITZ
SELECTED POEMS 1928-1958

History:

LEONARD D. WHITE & JEAN SCHNEIDER
THE REPUBLICAN ERA: 1869-1901

Journalism:

UTICA OBSERVER-DISPATCH; THE UTICA DAILY PRESS

National Reporting:

HOWARD VAN SMITH
MIAMI NEWS

International Reporting:

JOSEPH MARTIN & PHILIP SANTORA
THE NEW YORK DAILY NEWS

Editorial Cartooning:

BILL MAULDIN
ST. LOUIS POST-DISPATCH

Biography or Autobiography:

ARTHUR WALWORTH
WOODROW WILSON: AMERICAN PROPHET

A 15th Century Manuscript Of **Chaucer's "Canterbury Tales,"** Complete With Correction Marks, **Sells For $42,560** In London.

A Letter Written By **Martha Washington** In 1799 **Sells For $1,400** At A New York Auction.

WHAT A YEAR IT WAS!

1959
DISASTERS

38 People Die
From An Explosion Of Old World War II Bombs In Dagupan, Luzon.

95 People Perish
When "Unsinkable" Danish Passenger Ship "Hedtoft" Strikes An Iceberg And Sinks Off Cape Farewell, Greenland.

Elephant Rampage
At A Religious Festival In Kandy, Ceylon Kills 14 And Injures Many Others.

ENGLAND
A Fire In The Shopping Area Of Ilford, England Causes $42 Million In Property Damage.

AIRLINER CRASHES
Into New York's East River Killing 65.

31 PEOPLE DIE
As Airliner Disintegrates In The Air During Thunderstorm Near Baltimore, Maryland.

BUFFALO, TEXAS
Is The Site Of A Mid-Air Explosion Which Kills 34.

FLOODS, SLEET and BLIZZARDS
Sweep The East And Midwestern United States With 71 Dead And Thousands Left Homeless In 15 States. Property Damage Reaches Over $1 Million In Oswego, New York As Buildings Collapse After Continuous Snowstorms Drop A Total Of 80 Inches.

. . . .

Hurricanes And Floods Strike Colima And Jalisco States, Mexico Killing 1,452.

WHAT A YEAR IT WAS!

EXTRA!

Hollywood... In The Worst Fire In The City's History, 35 Houses Are Destroyed In Hollywood's Laurel Canyon.

Scotland... Fire Breaks Out In A Kirkintilloch, Scotland Coal Mine, Killing 47 People.

The Arkansas Negro Boys Industrial School Is The Site Of A Fire Killing 21 Boys.

971 People Die In The United States In Traffic Accidents Over The Four-Day Christmas And Four-Day New Year's Holidays.

GEORGIA

Nine children drown when their school bus goes out of control and plunges into a pond near Tifton, Georgia.

✤ The Vega de Tera Dam in Zamora Province, Spain collapses after 30 days of rain pouring 230 million cubic feet of water onto a sleeping village.

✤ Wisconsin suffers through its heaviest snowfall in 86 years.

✤ Tourists are trapped in rock and earth and some 28 lose their lives as the first earthquakes to hit West Yellowstone, Montana this century causes heavy landslides, moves mountains, creates new natural dams and does great damage to the Hebgen Dam.

More than 20 passengers die as a commuter train plunges through an open drawbridge in Newark Bay.

✤ Described as the worst typhoon in Japanese history, "Vera" sweeps through central Honshu killing 1,300 people with another 1,200 reported missing and 1,000,000 left homeless as 550,000 dwellings are destroyed.

Italy unveils its fashions for

This clever
3-piece
combination
includes top, pants
and matching
jacket.

La bella signorina starts the day ready for
anything in this chic daytime dress that with
a twist of the wrist lets her get into the swim
of things.

This Japanese
influenced outfit
decorated with
butterflies seems
appropriate since
Madame Butterfly
came from Italy.

swim, sun, fun

And for you gals who want to do a little hip trimming, this ruffled suit could do the trick.

Italian fashions have proven quite popular across the oceans.

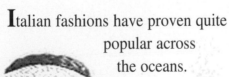

IT'S A WELL DRESSED FASHION WORLD

PARIS
The French fashion world is all agog over designer Jules Francois Crahay's first comprehensive collection for Nina Ricci, especially his plunging necklines and sensual curves.

MOSCOW
At the United States Exhibition, Muscovites get a glimpse of how average American adolescents dress. Jeans, sweaters and leather jackets make up some of the casual outfits.

NEGEV
Israeli fabrics continue to gain popularity in clothing designs.

LONDON
Hats with built in air-conditioning are available to avoid breathing unhealthy air.

NEW YORK
The Soviets send over some of their top designers with new creations.

LOS ANGELES
Teenagers make their own suits out of blankets.

FASHIONS *in* ENGLAND

DESIGNER NORMAN HARKNELL INTRODUCES HIS NEW LINE FOR FALL AND WINTER.

Traditional British strong points, woolens and tweeds, are very much in evidence in this beautiful suit.

This tweed suit with matching plaid coat, along with the entire collection, will be featured at the gala Scottish industry's exposition later this year.

Two more outfits in wool complete the show demonstrating British artistry at its finest.

Appropriately this stunning ball gown in pure silk satin (above) is richly embroidered with a motif of Scottish roses in gold and crystal.

Continuing the highland's theme, another evening dress in shirting material brightened with the MacBeth Tartan.

WHAT A YEAR IT WAS!

Maggie McNellis (left) Arlene Francis, escorted by Joseph Cotton (center) and Claudette Colbert and Charles Boyer (right) are among some of the stars participating in this very special event.

March Of Dimes Gala

On stage, one-half million dollars worth of the latest spring fashions are paraded by celebrities turned models.

Some 1,200 people crowd the grand ballroom at New York's Waldorf Astoria for the nation's most famous fashion show – the 15th annual edition of the March Of Dimes style event.

The real stars of the evening are the March Of Dimes poster children who are brought on stage by Jimmy Durante – a reminder that the purpose of this glamorous evening is the support of the foundation's fundraising for research against this crippling disease.

Gliding down the runway with grace and charm are the first lady of American Theatre, Helen Hayes (right) and the vivacious Celeste Holm (left).

WHAT A YEAR IT WAS!

155

1959

GOODBYE SACK DRESS, HELLO FASHIONS FAVORING THE FEMININE FIGURE.

Designer Gabrielle "Coco" Chanel once again proves her legendary status by creating some of the most talked about outfits of the season. Her classic suits appeal to women unconcerned with the latest fads. Chanel's influence is seen in designs from fashion houses throughout Europe and the U.S.

FASHION

A to Z

Americana Print
Brocade
Conical Sleeve
Dropped Shoulder
Envelope Handbag
Flannel
Gloves
Hobble Skirt
Italian Design

Jeweled Embroidery
Knit
Leotard
Mauve
Nylon Hose
Organdy
Pleat

Quality Fabric
Rickrack

Straw
Turquoise
Under-Collar Suit
Velcro
Wee Waist, Wide Belt
Xtreme Bosom
Yellow
Zefran

COTY
AMERICAN FASHION CRITICS' HALL OF FAME AWARD
James Galanos & Pauline Trigére

YVES ST. LAURENT—HEAD OF THE HOUSE OF DIOR

Eat, drink and be merry!
He allows his models to gain nearly 10 pounds to better show his new curvy clothes.

He breaks with other Parisian designers and raises hemlines to the knee area.

His knee-cinching skirts are controversial.

He has a fashion show in Moscow sending over 100 dresses, priced at $300 and up.

His vital importance to the fashion industry continues to be recognized by the French Government, and his entrance to the army is postponed until the fall of 1960.

WHAT A YEAR IT WAS!

Hat News

Hat designer Franny Whitney creates wire mobile hats, which, in addition to being perched on a lovely head, are also works of art. The whimsical hats can be seen at a New York gallery and have caught the eye of sculptor Alexander Calder, who declares, "I wish I'd done them myself."

Straw Hat Day is celebrated across the country and Pierre Cardin's straw hat is a big seller in high-fashion circles.

Fashionable hats include the Ballibuntl and Breton.

Veils move north and become hats in their own right.

1958 Winnie winner Arnold Scassi's costly creations sell from just under $200 to nearly $2,000.

What's A Jet-Setting Fashion Queen To Do? The New York Dress Institute retires Mrs. William Paley and the Duchess of Windsor from their best-dressed list and puts them both in their Hall of Fame.

The Fashion Police Is Watching...
A fashion spy is caught in Paris and sent to jail. The tip-off? Dozens and dozens of drawings are found of yet-to-be released designs from major and minor French fashion houses.

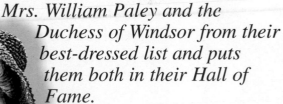

bikinis get smaller, grow bigger in popularity.

The waistline on Empire dresses moves up – to just under the bust

NEIMAN-MARCUS AWARD FOR DISTINGUISHED SERVICE
(a few of the many winners)
Anne Klein
Rosalind Russell
Arnold Scassi

Velveteen, denim, paisley cotton or Arnel sharkskin slacks gives the slender woman a respite from dresses and skirts.

A Los Angeles fashion presentation displays fashions for the blind modeled by the blind.

WHAT A YEAR IT WAS!

1959

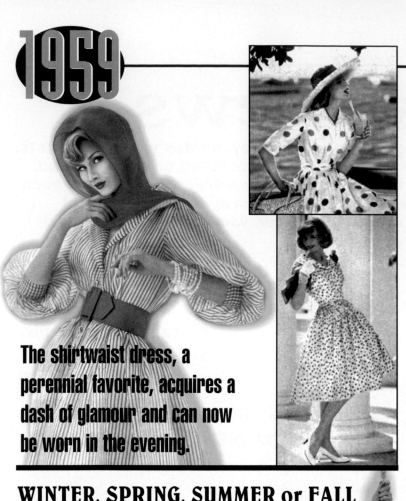

The shirtwaist dress, a perennial favorite, acquires a dash of glamour and can now be worn in the evening.

A short jacket over matching dress with long handbag, gloves and hat.

Silk dress with pleated skirt, a polka dot belt and scarf, sheer hose and low pumps.

WINTER, SPRING, SUMMER or FALL – Look Good Through Them All.

Winter: Short sleeve coat with oversized buttons.

Spring: Light blue chiffon blouse under hip-length jacket.

Summer: Cotton shirt and capri pants with an over-sized straw hat.

Fall: Wool jersey dress with a short jacket in wool or silk.

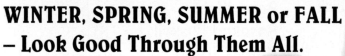

GIRLS ARE GIDDY OVER GINGHAM...

And wear dresses and bathing suits made of the checkered material.

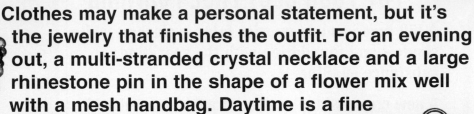

NIFTY KNICKKNACKS

Clothes may make a personal statement, but it's the jewelry that finishes the outfit. For an evening out, a multi-stranded crystal necklace and a large rhinestone pin in the shape of a flower mix well with a mesh handbag. Daytime is a fine time for a simple pearl necklace with matching bracelet and earrings.

Henry Fonda's pretty daughter **Jane** is a model for **"Vogue"** magazine.

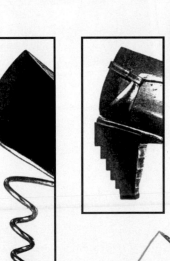

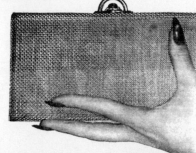

SHOES

Comfort in women's shoes is an important part of this year's footwear. Pointed toes and high heels give way to lower heels and rounded toes. Ankle boots with flat heels are worn with dresses and suits. A novel idea is the heel-free shoe, made for those who are light on their toes.

1959

PUT YOUR BEST FACE FORWARD

A '59 face is made up with false eyelashes, white shadow and foundation with the sparkling substance guanine.

A new cream with placenta extract is guaranteed to moisturize and revitalize your skin.

Ultra-Feminine, by Helena Rubenstein, is a moisturizer that has estrogen and progesterone as the key ingredients.

The Makeur is the mechanical way to put on make-up and creams with ease and accuracy.

The natural look is fine and dandy – as long as it's created with flattering make-up.

HAIR

Hair styles include the bouffant, soft waves, bangs, French twist and dips. Women begin growing their hair long, wearing it down or stacking it atop the head with jewelry. Those feeling nostalgic for yesteryear can try wearing their hair as Greta Garbo did decades ago.

IT'S WIGGY, MAN

Low-priced wigs in wild shades such as purple and red sell thousands a day.

WHAT A YEAR IT WAS!

MEN'S FASHIONS

The blucher and wing tip are two ways to top the toes.

The bowler hat is back on top.

The single-breasted Continental suit gains in popularity, giving the Ivy look competition. Wash and Wear suits become more affordable than ever before.

Indian madras is an excellent choice for a lightweight sports coat.

A SURREY WITH THE FRINGE ON TOP...

Sears, Roebuck & Company joins the toupee business, and offers its male customers a varied selection of quality rugs in the $200 range.

Britain's "Tailor and Cutter" magazine chooses an eclectic and international group of men for their yearly best-dressed list. Fred Astaire, Marshall Tito, Richard Nixon and Rex Harrison are among those whose tailored togs keep them looking snappy. At the other end of the spectrum another British magazine, "Man About Town," lists musicians Liberace and Elvis Presley as amongst the world's worst-dressed fellas.

MAX FACTOR whips up Creme Puff

always ready to flatter your face
with just a breath of color

Only compact make-up with shades so delicately blended they match each individual complexion. Creme Puff never changes on your face. Ends "Color-Patching" forever!

Just the breath of color you desire! It's *yours*, any time... any place with Creme Puff by MAX FACTOR! You have your choice of nine true-skin tones—blended for each type of complexion as only MAX FACTOR can. Other compact make-ups combine with skin oils... start "color-patching." But Creme Puff is such a perfectly balanced blend of creamy make-up base and sheerest powder—it *ends "color-patching" forever!*

IVORY COMPACT...1.25* GOLD-TONE COMPACT...2.25*
REFILS...ONLY 85¢*   *PLUS TAX

MAX FACTOR...*Master of Make-Up Artistry For 50 Years*

©1959, MAX FACTOR & CO.

SPORTS

The Pennant Comes To Chicago As The White Sox Play In The World Series For The First Time In 40 Years.

In The Sixth Game Los Angeles Explodes With Duke Snider's Third Inning Homer For A 2-0 Lead.

On The Mound To Finish It Off For The Dodgers Is Larry Sherry Who Is Involved In All Four Los Angeles Victories.

From Seventh Place Last Season, The Dodgers Rebounded To The Top And Win The World Series Beating The White Sox 4-2, The First Team In Major League History To Make Such A Dramatic Comeback.

1959 Baseball

FOR THE FIRST TIME IN MAJOR LEAGUE HISTORY, TWO ALL-STAR GAMES ARE PLAYED For The Benefit Of The Players' Pension Fund With The National League Beating The American League 5-4 In The First Game And The American League Getting Even In The Second Winning 5-3.

Most Valuable Player
National League:
Ernie Banks (Chicago)
American League:
Nellie Fox (Chicago)

ROOKIE OF THE YEAR
NATIONAL LEAGUE
WILLIE McCOVEY (SAN FRANCISCO)
AMERICAN LEAGUE
BOB ALLISON (WASHINGTON)

CY YOUNG AWARD WINNER
EARLY WYNN (WHITE SOX)

SEASON HOME RUN KINGS
NATIONAL LEAGUE
ED MATHEWS (MILWAUKEE 46 HOME RUNS)
AMERICAN LEAGUE
ROCKY COLAVITO (CLEVELAND 42 HOME RUNS)
HARMON KILLEBREW (WASHINGTON 42 HOME RUNS)

BATTING CHAMPIONS
NATIONAL LEAGUE
HANK AARON (MILWAUKEE .355 AVERAGE)
AMERICAN LEAGUE
HARVEY KUENN (DETROIT .353 AVERAGE)

- Candlestick Park Is Officially Selected As The Name Of The Giants' New Ballpark In San Francisco.

- Dodgers Pitcher **Sandy Koufax** Ties Bob Feller's Single Game Strike Out Record And Sets New Two-Game Record.

- **Branch Rickey** Named President Of The Newly Formed Continental League, Baseball's Third Major League.

- Los Angeles Dedicates New Sports Arena Adjacent To Memorial Coliseum.

- Pittsburgh Pitcher **Harvey Haddix** Throws A 12-Inning Perfect Game Against The Milwaukee Braves.

The Martians Are Coming, The Martians Are Coming

Boston White Sox owner, Bill Veeck, stages a mock martian helicopter landing and "abduction" of Nellie Fox and Luis Aparicio at Chicago's Comiskey Park.

Some Days You Just Shouldn't Get Out Of Bed

Cincinnati pitcher Willard Schmidt is forced to leave a game against the Milwaukee Braves after being hit by two pitches, one batted ball and finally a line drive.

PASSINGS
Owner of the unmatched pitching record of 464 innings in one season, baseball Hall of Fame member **Ed Walsh** dies at age 78.

Napoleon "Larry" Lajoie, baseball Hall of Famer and greatest second baseman in history, dies at 83.

WHAT A YEAR IT WAS!

10,000 fans turn out in Indianapolis to watch heavyweight champion **Floyd Patterson** slash away at his fourth challenger Britain's **Brian London**.

In the 9th round a thunderous barrage of body blows brings down London's guard and cracks open the defense of the 10-1 underdog.

Late in the 10th round, London goes down on one knee after a smashing right high on the cheek but the bell rings on the count of 5 saving the challenger.

Trainers revive London after the round 10 knock down.

London is under blistering fire and a smashing hook drives him across the ring for the K.O. in the 11th round.

BOXING
WORLD TITLES

HEAVYWEIGHT
INGEMAR JOHANSSON
Johansson knocks down current champ, Floyd Patterson, seven times in the third round winning the heavyweight title.

MIDDLEWEIGHT
GENE FULLMER

WELTERWEIGHT
VIRGIL AKINS
DON JORDAN

LIGHT-HEAVYWEIGHT
ARCHIE MOORE

LIGHTWEIGHT
JOE BROWN

— PASSINGS —
Former Heavyweight champ, **Max Baer**, dies at 50.

Tony Canzoneri, holder of world championships in three weight divisions (Jr. Welterweight, Featherweight and Lightweight), dies at 51.

CASSIUS CLAY fights his first amateur bouts.

Bowling

WHAT A YEAR IT WAS!

AMERICAN BOWLING CONGRESS CHAMPION
All Events: **Ed Lubanski** Detroit, Michigan
2,116 points.

WOMEN'S INTERNATIONAL BOWLING CONGRESS CHAMPION
All Events: **Pat McBride** Grand Rapids, Michigan
Scores 1,927 points, breaking a 25-year old record.

1959

BASKETBALL

The East (Dark) Takes On The West (White) In The 9th NBA All-Star Game Played In Detroit.

Minneapolis Rookie Elgin Baylor Shows A Play That Entitles Him To Share In The Outstanding Player Award For This Game.

1.

The Favored East Fights Back As Boston's Bob Cousy Gets The Ball And Despite A Leg Injury Is In Great Form.

2.

3.

Cousy's Shot Hits The Rim But Bill Russell, Another Celtic, Taps It In.

Later In The Game, Cousy Steals The Ball From Slater Martin Of St. Louis And Scores Again.

4.

The West Pulls Off A Late Rally With Pettit's Long Pass To Jack Twyman For An Easy Lay-Up And Wins 124-108.

5.

AUTO RACING

WORLD GRAND PRIX CHAMPION
JACK BRABHAM (Australia)

WINSTON CUP CHAMPION
LEE PETTY

INDIANAPOLIS 500 WINNER
RODGER WARD
driving a Leader Card Special 500 Roadster at average speed of 135.857 mph collects $106,850 cash prize.

166

WHAT A YEAR IT WAS!

BASKETBALL

NATIONAL BASKETBALL ASSOCIATION CHAMPIONS
Captain Bob Cousy Leads Boston Celtics To Championship Beating Minneapolis Lakers 4-0.

NBA MOST VALUABLE PLAYER
Bob Pettit
(St. Louis)

N.C.A.A. TITLE
Golden Bears Edge West Virginia 71-70 Giving The Pacific Coast Conference Its First Win Since 1942.

NBA ROOKIE OF THE YEAR
Elgin Baylor
(Minneapolis)

NBA SCORING CHAMPION
Bob Pettit
(St. Louis)

Wilt Chamberlain wins Golden State rookie award.

Elgin Baylor refuses to play in Charleston when a hotel turns away Negro teammates.

NBA adopts protective policy that demands hosting city not practice segregation of any of its players.

CHESS

WORLD CHESS CHAMPIONSHIP
Mikhail Botvinnik, USSR

America's 16-Year Old Champion **Bobby Fischer** Finishes Fifth In The Final Standing In The World Challenger's Chess Tournament Held In Yugoslavia.

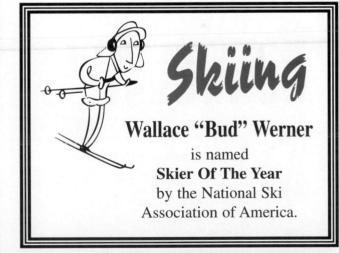

Skiing

Wallace "Bud" Werner is named **Skier Of The Year** by the National Ski Association of America.

ICE SKATING

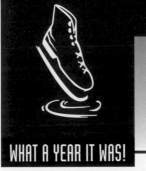

WORLD FIGURE SKATING CHAMPIONS

Men: Dave Jenkins (U.S.)

Women: Carol Heiss (U.S.)

WHAT A YEAR IT WAS!

1959 *FOOTBALL*

BALTIMORE COLTS Beat **NEW YORK GIANTS** 31-16 Winning **National Football League Championship**

PROFESSIONAL PLAYER OF THE YEAR

JOHNNY UNITAS QB, Baltimore Colts

National College Football Champion **SYRACUSE**

Heisman Trophy Winner **BILLY CANNON** (HB) LSU

Army and **Air Force** kick off their rivalry in New York's Yankee Stadium going head to head in a 13-13 tie with 67,000 fans rooting for their favorite.

Over 98,000 fans watch as **Iowa** beats **California** 38-12 winning the **Rose Bowl** championship.

NCAA RULE CHANGES

Increase the space between the goal posts by 4′ 10″ to a total width of 23′ 4″.

Increase the number of allowable time-outs from four to five in each half.

NATIONAL FOOTBALL LEAGUE'S MANAGER OF THE YEAR
Vince Lombardi

Lamar Hunt forms the American Football League.

William "Billy" Sullivan buys Boston Patriots, an AFL franchise, for $25,000.

The Buffalo Bills become the American Football League's seventh team when franchise is awarded to Ralph C. Wilson.

PASSINGS
One of the people responsible for making football a major spectator sport due to his profitable television policies, Bert Bell, former commissioner of the NFL, dies at 65.

SOCCER
The **McIllane Canvasbacks** of San Pedro, California win the United States Challenge Cup beating the **Fall River Massachusetts** team 4-3.

WHAT A YEAR IT WAS!

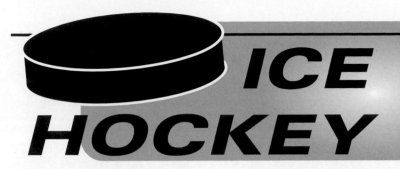
ICE HOCKEY

STANLEY CUP

Montreal Canadiens Beat Toronto Maple Leafs 4-1 For Win.

CALDER MEMORIAL
(Rookie Of The Year)
RALPH BACKSTROM
Montreal

ART ROSS TROPHY
(Leading Scorer)
DICKIE MOORE
Montreal

LADY BYNG MEMORIAL TROPHY
(Most Gentlemanly Player)
ALEX DELVECCHIO
Detroit

HART MEMORIAL TROPHY
(Most Valuable Player)
ANDY BATHGATE
N.Y. Rangers

VEZINA TROPHY
(Outstanding Goalie)
JACQUES PLANTE
Montreal
(wins for fourth straight time)

They Wear Parachutes When Jumping Out Of Planes, Don't They?

After being hit in the face with a puck during a game against the New York Rangers in New York's Madison Square Garden, Montreal Canadiens' Jacques Plante shocks fans by returning to the ice wearing a face mask which he designed himself, becoming the first goalie to do so during a regular season game.

GOLF
CHAMPIONS

Professional Golfers Association
Bob Rosburg

Ladies Professional Golfers Association
Betsy Rawls

Women's National Amateur
Barbara McIntire

British Open
Gary Player
(Youngest winner in modern history)

Masters
Art Wall, Jr.
(Wins by one stroke with 72-hole score of 284)

U.S. Amateur
Jack Nicklaus
(Youngest winner in 50 years)

U.S. Open
MEN: **Billy Casper**
WOMEN: **Mary Kathryn "Mickey" Wright**
(Sets record by winning title two years in a row)

LEADING PROFESSIONAL MONEY WINNER
ART WALL, JR. (Approximately $50,000)

• After winning 63 tournaments over thirty years golfing legend **Ben Hogan** retires.

• The U.S. retains the Walker Cup defeating the British amateurs 9-3 in Scotland.

WHAT A YEAR IT WAS!

WILLIE SHOEMAKER Rides TOMY LEE To Kentucky Derby Win.

HORSE OF THE YEAR: Sword Dancer (with Eddie Arcaro usually riding, Sword Dancer is #1 earner at $537,004.)

HARNESS HORSE OF THE YEAR: Bye Bye Bird

Turf history is made at Churchill Downs with the sensational finish of the Kentucky Derby.

Tomy Lee and Sword Dancer engage in one of the greatest home stretch duels ever producing the only foul claim in Derby history. Tomy Lee wins the run for the roses.

Track & Field Sensation Of The Year

is the 7′ 1-1/4″ high jump of **John Curtis Thomas** at Madison Square Garden.

The 17-year old Boston University freshman beams as he sets a dazzling new world record.

James E. Sullivan
Memorial Trophy
Awarded For
Outstanding Sportsmanship
Parry O'Brien (Track)

170

WHAT A YEAR IT WAS!

171

TENNIS

CHAMPIONS

U.S. OPEN (SINGLES)
Men: Neal A. Fraser (over Alejandro Olmedo)
Women: Maria Bueno (over Christine Truman)

WIMBLEDON
Men: Alejandro Olmedo (over Rod Laver)
Women: Maria Bueno (over Darlene Hard)

DAVIS CUP
In the deciding game played in Forest Hills, New York, Australia's Neale Fraser beats America's Barry MacKay 3-2 regaining the Davis Cup.

12-Year Old Romanian Ilie Nastase, Wins National Boys' Title.

PASSINGS
Tennis Hall of Fame member and record 8-time winner of the U.S. Women's Singles, Molla Bjurstedt Mallory, dies at 67.

FAMOUS BIRTHS

Danny Ainge
•
Earvin "Magic" Johnson
•
Florence Griffith Joyner
•
Ronnie Lott
•
John McEnroe
•
Jim McMahon

Cycling
Amateur Bicycle League of America Championships

Men's Senior Open Title
James Rossi, Chicago

Women's Open Title
Joanne Speckin, Detroit

Tour de France
Spain's **Federico Bahamontes** wins Europe's blue-ribbon event.

Badminton

Men's Singles Title
Tan Joe Hok
(Indonesia)

Women's Singles Title
Judy Devlin
(USA)

WHAT A YEAR IT WAS!

1959

Pan-American Games

Swimming

15-year old Susan "Chris" von Saltza of Los Gatos High School in Santa Clara, California wins five gold medals.

Marathon

Groton, Connecticut teacher John Kelley scores outstanding victory.

Basketball

Men: United States
Women: United States

Gymnastics

Men:
(all around)
John Beckner, U. S.
(114.3 pts.)

Women:
(all around)
Ernestine Russell, Canada
(38.467 pts.)

Volleyball

Men: United States
Women: Brazil

Wrestling

AMATEUR ATHLETIC NATIONAL CHAMPIONS: Bill Kerslake keeps heavyweight crown and Terry McCann keeps the crown in the 125.5 lb. class.

Yachting

Peter Grant's "Nalu II," a 46-ft. sloop, wins the Transpacific race from Los Angeles, California to Honolulu, Hawaii.

Table Tennis

New York City's Bobby Gusikoff defeats Marty Reisman winning U. S. National Open Table Tennis championship and Susie Hoshi defeats Sharon Acton in the women's division.

New York City's Westminster Club Top Dog Award goes to Miniature Poodle champion **Fontclair Festoon**.

Anne Hone Rogers becomes first woman dog trainer to twice win the Westminster Kennel Club's Best Dog ribbon when her black Miniature Poodle **Tina** takes first prize.

Bobsledding

The United States gets its first international crown since 1950 when **ART TYLER** of Boston pilots his four-man sled to top honors in St. Moritz, Switzerland.

SIR HUGH STOCKWELL Wins The World's **tiddlywinks** Championship In London.

PASSINGS

Perhaps the greatest billiards player in the history of the game, Willie Hoppe dies at age 71. He won his first championship at age 18 and was the three-cushion champion for nearly a half century.

WHAT A YEAR IT WAS!

1959 WAS A GREAT YEAR, BUT...

THE BEST IS YET TO COME!